MW00583849

Learn German with Science Fiction To the Zero Point of Existence

HypLern Interlinear Project
www.hyplern.com

First edition: 2021, March

Author: Kurd Laßwitz
Translation: Kees van den End
Foreword: Camilo Andrés Bonilla Carvajal PhD

Translation and interlinear formatting © 2021 Bermuda Word. All rights reserved.

ISBN: 978-1-989643-32-7

kees@hyplern.com
www.hyplern.com

Learn German with Science Fiction
To the Zero Point of Existence

Interlinear German to English

Author
Kurd Laßwitz

Translation
Kees van den End

HypLern Interlinear Project
www.hyplern.com

The HypLern Method

Learning a foreign language should not mean leafing through page after page in a bilingual dictionary until one's fingertips begin to hurt. Quite the contrary, through everyday language use, friendly reading, and direct exposure to the language we can get well on our way towards mastery of the vocabulary and grammar needed to read native texts. In this manner, learners can be successful in the foreign language without too much study of grammar paradigms or rules. Indeed, Seneca expresses in his sixth epistle that "Longum iter est per praecepta, breve et efficax per exempla[1]."

The HypLern series constitutes an effort to provide a highly effective tool for experiential foreign language learning. Those who are genuinely interested in utilizing original literary works to learn a foreign language do not have to use conventional graded texts or adapted versions for novice readers. The former only distort the actual essence of literary works, while the latter are highly reduced in vocabulary and relevant content. This collection aims to bring the lively experience of reading stories as directly told by their very authors to foreign language learners.

Most excited adult language learners will at some point seek their teachers' guidance on the process of learning to read in the foreign language rather than seeking out external opinions. However, both teachers and learners lack a general reading technique or strategy. Oftentimes, students undertake the reading task equipped with nothing more than a bilingual dictionary, a grammar book, and lots of courage. These efforts often end in frustration as the student builds mis-constructed nonsensical sentences after many hours spent on an aimless translation drill.

Consequently, we have decided to develop this series of interlinear translations intended to afford a comprehensive edition of unabridged texts. These texts are presented as they were originally written with no changes in word choice or order. As a result, we have a translated piece conveying the true meaning under every word from the original work. Our readers receive then two books in just one volume: the original version and its translation.

The reading task is no longer a laborious exercise of patiently decoding unclear and seemingly complex paragraphs. What's more, reading becomes an enjoyable and meaningful process of cultural, philosophical and linguistic learning. Independent learners can then acquire expressions and vocabulary while understanding pragmatic and socio-cultural dimensions of the target language by reading in it rather than reading about it.

Our proposal, however, does not claim to be a novelty. Interlinear translation is as old as the Spanish tongue, e.g. "glosses of [Saint] Emilianus", interlinear bibles in Old German, and of course James Hamilton's work in the 1800s. About the latter, we remind the readers, that as a revolutionary freethinker he promoted the publication of Greco-Roman classic works and further pieces in diverse languages. His effort, such as ours, sought to lighten the exhausting task of looking words up in large glossaries as an educational practice: "if there is any thing which fills reflecting men with melancholy and regret, it is the waste of mortal time, parental money, and puerile happiness, in the present method of pursuing Latin and Greek[2]".

Additionally, another influential figure in the same line of thought as Hamilton was John Locke. Locke was also the philosopher and translator of the Fabulae AEsopi in an interlinear plan. In 1600, he was already suggesting that interlinear texts, everyday communication, and use of the target language could be the most appropriate ways to achieve language learning:

> ...the true and genuine Way, and that which I would propose, not only as the easiest and best, wherein a Child might, without pains or Chiding, get a Language which others are wont to be whipt for at School six or seven Years together...[3]

---

1 "The journey is long through precepts, but brief and effective through examples". Seneca, Lucius Annaeus. (1961) Ad Lucilium Epistulae Morales, vol. I. London: W. Heinemann.

2 In: Hamilton, James (1829?) History, principles, practice and results of the Hamiltonian system, with answers to the Edinburgh and Westminster reviews; A lecture delivered at Liverpool; and instructions for the use of the books published on the system. Londres: W. Aylott and Co., 8, Pater Noster Row. p. 29.

3 In: Locke, John. (1693) Some thoughts concerning education. Londres: A. and J. Churchill. pp. 196-7.

Who can benefit from this edition?

We identify three kinds of readers, namely, those who take this work as a search tool, those who want to learn a language by reading authentic materials, and those attempting to read writers in their original language. The HypLern collection constitutes a very effective instrument for all of them.

1. For the first target audience, this edition represents a search tool to connect their mother tongue with that of the writer's. Therefore, they have the opportunity to read over an original literary work in an enriching and certain manner.
2. For the second group, reading every word or idiomatic expression in its actual context of use will yield a strong association between the form, the collocation, and the context. This will have a direct impact on long term learning of passive vocabulary, gradually building genuine reading ability in the original language. This book is an ideal companion not only to independent learners but also to those who take lessons with a teacher. At the same time, the continuous feeling of achievement produced during the process of reading original authors both stimulates and empowers the learner to study[1].
3. Finally, the third kind of reader will notice the same benefits as the previous ones. The proximity of a word and its translation in our interlinear texts is a step further from other collections, such as the Loeb Classical Library. Although their works might be considered the most famous in this genre, the presentation of texts on opposite pages hinders the immediate link between words and their semantic equivalence in our native tongue (or one we have a strong mastery of).

---

1 Some further ways of using the present work include:

1. As you progress through the stories, focus less on the lower line (the English translation). Instead, try to read through the upper line, staying in the foreign language as long as possible.
2. Even if you find glosses or explanatory footnotes about the mechanics of the language, you should make your own hypotheses on word formation and syntactical functions in a sentence. Feel confident about inferring your own language rules and test them progressively. You can also take notes concerning those idiomatic expressions or special language usage that calls your attention for later study.
3. As soon as you finish each text, check the reading in the original version (with no interlinear or parallel translation). This will fulfil the main goal of this collection: bridging the gap between readers and original literary works, training them to read directly and independently.

Why interlinear?

Conventionally speaking, tiresome reading in tricky and exhausting circumstances has been the common definition of learning by texts. This collection offers a friendly reading format where the language is not a stumbling block anymore. Contrastively, our collection presents a language as a vehicle through which readers can attain and understand their authors' written ideas.

While learning to read, most people are urged to use the dictionary and distinguish words from multiple entries. We help readers skip this step by providing the proper translation based on the surrounding context. In so doing, readers have the chance to invest energy and time in understanding the text and learning vocabulary; they read quickly and easily like a skilled horseman cantering through a book.

Thereby we stress the fact that our proposal is not new at all. Others have tried the same before, coming up with evident and substantial outcomes. Certainly, we are not pioneers in designing interlinear texts. Nonetheless, we are nowadays the only, and doubtless, the best, in providing you with interlinear foreign language texts.

Handling instructions

Using this book is very easy. Each text should be read at least three times in order to explore the whole potential of the method. The first phase is devoted to comparing words in the foreign language to those in the mother tongue. This is to say, the upper line is contrasted to the lower line as the following example shows:

Man	sah	sich	genötigt,	die	Wohnhäuser	in	so	gewaltigen
One	saw	oneself	compelled	the	residential houses	in	such	enormous

Dimensionen	aufzutürmen	und	die	Gärten	über	ihnen
dimensions	to tower up	and	the	gardens	over	them
	to pile up				on top of	

anzubringen,	da	man	den	Raum	der	ebenen	Erde	dem
on-to-bring to locate	since	one	the	space	of the	flat earth's surface	ground	the

Ackerbau	vorbehalten	musste.
agriculture	reserved	had to (be)

The second phase of reading focuses on capturing the meaning and sense of the original text. As readers gain practice with the method, they should be able to focus on the target language without getting distracted by the translation. New users of the method, however, may find it helpful to cover the translated lines with a piece of paper as illustrated in the image below. Subsequently, they try to understand the meaning of every word, phrase, and entire sentences in the target language itself, drawing on the translation only when necessary. In this phase, the reader should resist the temptation to look at the translation for every word. In doing so, they will find that they are able to understand a good portion of the text by reading directly in the target language, without the crutch of the translation. This is the skill we are looking to train: the ability to read and understand native materials and enjoy them as native speakers do, that being, directly in the original language.

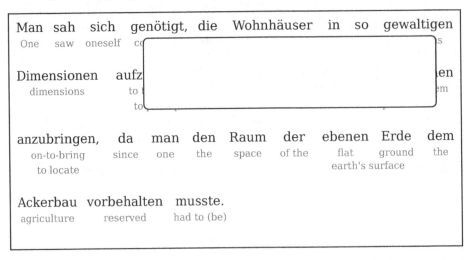

In the final phase, readers will be able to understand the meaning of the text when reading it without additional help. There may be some less common words and phrases which have not cemented themselves yet in the reader's brain, but the majority of the story should not pose any problems. If desired, the reader can use an SRS or some other memorization method to learning these straggling words.

> Man sah sich genötigt, die Wohnhäuser in so gewaltigen Dimensionen aufzutürmen und die Gärten über ihnen anzubringen, da man den Raum der ebenen Erde dem Ackerbau vorbehalten musste.

Above all, readers will not have to look every word up in a dictionary to read a text in the foreign language. This otherwise wasted time will be spent concentrating on their principal interest. These new readers will tackle authentic texts while learning their vocabulary and expressions to use in further communicative (written or oral) situations. This book is just one work from an overall series with the same purpose. It really helps those who are afraid of having "poor vocabulary" to feel confident about reading directly in the language. To all of them and to all of you, welcome to the amazing experience of living a foreign language!

Additional tools

Check out shop.hyplern.com or contact us at info@hyplern.com for free mp3s (if available) and free empty (untranslated) versions of the eBooks that we have on offer.

For some of the older eBooks and paperbacks we have Windows, iOS and Android apps available that, next to the interlinear format, allow for a pop-up format, where hovering over a word or clicking on it gives you its meaning. The apps also have any mp3s, if available, and integrated vocabulary practice.

Visit the site hyplern.com for the same functionality online. This is where we will be working non-stop to make all our material available in multiple formats, including audio where available, and vocabulary practice.

Table of Contents

Das Geruchsklavier

The Smell-piano

Aromasia saß im Garten ihres Hauses und sah
Aromasia sat in the garden of her house and saw

träumerisch ins Blau des schönen Sommertages vom
dreamily in the blue of the beautiful summer day from the

Jahre 2371. Sie folgte mit ihren Blicken den kleinen
years 2371. she followed with her glance the small

dunklen Wolken, welche sich hier und da plötzlich in
dark clouds which themselves here and there suddenly in

der Atmosphäre bildeten und einen Regenguss herabströmen
the atmosphere built and a downpour flow down

ließen; oder sie spähte nach den fliegenden Wagen und
let or she spied after the flying cart and

Luftvelozipeden aus, die zu ihren Füßen in buntem
air-bicycles ~~out~~ which at her feet in colorful

Gewühle die breite Straße erfüllten. Denn der Garten
bustle the wide street filled. Then / Because the garden

Aromasias befand sich in der luftigen Höhe von ungefähr
of Aromasia found itself in the airy . height of about

hundert Metern über dem Erdboden auf dem Dache ihres
hundred meter over the earth-floor / ground on the roof of her

Hauses.
house

1

Man sah sich genötigt, die Wohnhäuser in so
One saw oneself compelled the residential houses in such

gewaltigen Dimensionen aufzutürmen und die Gärten über
enormous dimensions to tower up / to pile up and the gardens over / on top of

ihnen anzubringen, da man den Raum der ebenen Erde
them on-to-bring / to locate since one the space of the flat ground / earth's surface

dem Ackerbau vorbehalten musste. So reich bevölkert war
the agriculture reserved had to (be) So rich populated was

der Erdball, dass man jedes Plätzchen dem Anbau der
the earth-ball / globe that one each little place the cultivation of the

Halmfrucht und der Ernährung des Schlachtviehs widmen
semolina and the nutrition of the slaughter cattle dedicate

musste, um die Gefahr einer Hungersnot abzuwenden.
must for the danger of a famine to avert

So wogten denn am Boden die Getreidefelder, wo
So swayed then at the ground the grain fields where

immer Luft und Licht es gestatteten; darüber standen auf
ever air and light it allowed there-above stood on

festen, hohen Säulen die Gebäude der Menschen, in
firm high columns the buildings of the people in

deren unteren Stockwerken die Industrie ihr geschäftiges
whose lower floors the industry her busy

Leben trieb. Weiter oben folgten Privatwohnungen, und die
life drove / had Further above followed private apartments and the

Krone des Ganzen bildeten anmutige Gärten, deren
crown of the whole (thing) built graceful gardens whose

freie und gesunde Lage sie zum beliebtesten Aufenthalte
free and healthy location them to the most popular stays

machte.
made

Die Aufeinanderfolge von fünfzehn bis fünfundzwanzig
The succession of fifteen to twenty five

Stockwerken war übrigens durchaus nicht mit
floors was by the way throughout not with
at all

Unbequemlichkeiten verbunden; denn der Luftwagen war
inconveniences connected then the air car was
because

das gewöhnliche Verkehrsmittel; und wollte man wirklich
the ordinary means of transport and wanted one really

einmal zu Fuß ausgehen, so fanden sich die Treppen
once on foot go out so found oneself the stairs
so

durch treffliche Hebe- und Senkvorrichtungen ersetzt. In
through excellent raise and sink-devices replaced in

den Städten – und deren gab es unzählige – waren
the cities – and (of) those gave it countless – were
were there

außerdem die einzelnen Stockwerke längs der Straßenfront
In addition the single floors along the street front

durch Galerien verbunden; ihre Benutzung war bequem
through galleries connected her use was comfortable

3

und praktisch, aber – wie es so geht, man weiß nicht
and practical but – as it so goes one know not

immer, warum – bei der feinen Gesellschaft galt sie
always why – at the delicate company was seen she
society

nicht für standesgemäß; sie diente nur dem kleinen
not for befitting she served only the small
as

Geschäftsverkehr und Hausgebrauche. Ebenso hielt man es
business transactions and home use Likewise held one it

für unpassend, ja, es war sogar straßenpolizeilich verboten,
for inappropriate yes it was even by the street police forbidden

innerhalb der Stadt mit den leichten Fahrzeugen sich
within the city with the light vehicles oneself

höher als die Dächer der Häuser zu erheben oder quer
higher than the roofs of the houses to raise or straight

über Privatbesitz durch die Luft zu fliegen. Natürlich
over private property through the air to fly Of course

gab es auch immer mutwillige und unartige Übertreter
gave it also always wanton and naughty trespassers
were there

dieser Sitte, und wenn es früher, im rohen
of this habit, and when it before, in the raw

Neu-Mittelalter, der Übermut der männlichen Jugend nicht
new middle ages the high spirits of the male youth not

verschmähte, in weinseliger Nacht allerlei Unfug an
spurned in more palatable night all kinds of nonsense on

Schildern und Hausklingeln zu verüben, so kam
painting and doorbells to perpetrate so came
graffiti {kam for: happened}

4

es   auch   heute   wohl   vor,   dass   sich   am   Morgen   ein
it   also   today   well   before   that   itself   at the / in the   morning   a

Fenster   mit   schönen   Bildern   verklebt   fand   oder   ein
window   with   beautiful   pictures   glued   found   or   a

wohlverpacktes   Bukett   zum   Schornstein   hereinspazierte.
well packed   bouquet   to the   chimney   walked in / fell in

Aromasia   Duftemann   Ozodes,   die   allverehrte   Künstlerin,
Aromasia   Duftemann {Fragrantman}   Ozodes   the   dear   artist

seufzte   leise,   nachdem   sie   wieder   vergebens   in   der   Menge
sighed   softly   after   she   again   in vain   in   the   mass

der   Luft-Droschken   nach   dem   Ziele   ihrer   Sehnsucht
of the   little air carriages   after   the   target   of her   desire

gesucht   hatte.
sought   had

»Wo   nur   Oxygen   bleiben   mag?«,   klagte   sie   sanft   in
Where   only   Oxygen   stay   may   complained   she   softly   in
What's keeping Oxygen

den   wohltönenden   Lauten   der   deutschen   Sprache.   Denn
the   soothing   ring   of the   German   language   Then

wenn   man   auch   im   gewöhnlichen   Verkehre   sich   fast
when   one   also   in the   normal   traffic   oneself   almost

ausschließlich   der   neu   eingeführten   Universalsprache   zu
exclusively   the   new   introduced   universal language   to

bedienen   pflegte,   so   sprach   man   doch   die   zarten
serve   used   so   spoke   one   indeed   the   gentle

Empfindungen des Herzens in den süßen Klängen der
sensations of the heart in the sweet sounds of the

ursprünglichen Muttersprache aus.
original mother tongue ~~out~~

»Merkwürdig«, fuhr sie fort, »dass er nicht nach seiner
Strange drove she away that he not after his
continued she

Gewohnheit längst zu mir geeilt. Schon neun Uhr
habits already long to me hurried (is) Already nine hour

vierundachtzig Minuten siebzig Sekunden? Man teilte den
eighty-four minutes seventy seconds One shared the

Tag in zweimal zehn Stunden à 100 Minuten à 100
day in twice ten hours at 100 minutes at 100

Sekunden.
seconds

Und auch Magnet kommt nicht – aber die Dichter sind
And also Magnet comes not – but the poets are

unpünktlich. Er sinnt gewiss auf ein Grunzulett; und
unpunctual He ponders certainly on a greentreat and

dazu braucht er Zeit.«
there-to needs he time

Das Grunzulett ist nämlich eine neue Dichtungsform,
The greentreat is namely a new form of poem

welche die Vorzüge des Sonetts, des Gasels, der
which the benefits of the sonnets of the gasels the

alcäischen Strophe und des Familienromans in sich
alcaean verse and of the family novel in itself

6

vereinigt, leider aber nur in der modernen
unites unfortunately however only in the modern

Universalsprache zu leisten ist, weil seine Hauptschönheit
universal language to succeed is because its main beauty

darin besteht, dass Alliteration und Reim durch eigene
therein exists that alliteration and rhyme through own

Selbstvernichtung sich zu einer neuen Form, der »in
self-destruction themselves to a new form the in

sich zurückkehrenden unendlichen Lautquetsche«, verbinden.
itself returning infinite sound-squeeze connect

Jetzt griff Aromasia nach dem neben ihr liegenden
Now grabbed Aromasia to the beside her laying

Doppelfernrohr und sah scharf nach einer Stelle der
double telescope and saw sharp to a spot of the

Vorstadt, welche ungefähr 25 Kilometer von ihrem
suburb which about 25 kilometers from her

Standpunkte entfernt sein mochte; eine jener schon
viewpoints removed be might one of those already

erwähnten kleinen Wolken erhob sich gerade darüber.
mentioned small clouds raised itself just there-over
                                                     above it

»Es ist Oxygen«, sagte sie beruhigt bei sich, indem sie
It is Oxygen said she calmed down by herself while she

das Fernrohr sinken ließ. »Ich erkenne seine Maschine.
the telescope sink let I recognize his machine

Er ist also beschäftigt und wird erst später erscheinen. So
He is thus occupied and will first later appear So
So he is

7

muss ich mir denn bis zu seiner Ankunft die Zeit nach
must I myself then until to his arrival the time to

eigenem Geschmack vertreiben. Wohlauf, meine getreue
(my) own taste drive out / pass Well my faithful

Kunst! Ihr gewaltigen Gedanken der großen Duftmeister
art You enormous thoughts of the great fragrance master

sollt mir die schleichende Stunde verkürzen und meine
should me the creeping hour shorten and my

Seele in die Regionen wunschlosen Wahnes tragen!«
soul in the regions of the wishless madness carry

Sie trat auf die Versenkung und befand sich wenige
She stepped on the sinking (apparatus) and found herself (a) few

Augenblicke später in ihrem geschmackvoll eingerichteten
moments later in her tastefully decorated

Zimmer. Ein Instrument in der Gestalt eines Pianinos
room An instrument in the shape of a small piano

stand in der Mitte. Sie öffnete den Deckel und griff in
stood in the middle She opened the cover and grabbed in

die Klaviatur des Ododions; bald schwelgte sie in den
the keyboard of the Ododions soon reveled she in the

Wonnedüften einer Fantasie von Riechmann, und
delightful scents a fantasy of Riechmann {smell-man} and

harmonische Wohlgerüche durchströmten das Zimmer.
harmonious fragrances flowed through the room

Das Ododion (von οδωδη, der Geruch) oder Geruchsklavier
The Ododion from ododi {greek} the smell or Smell-piano

wurde im Jahre 2094 von einem Italiener namens
became in the years 2094 from by an Italian of the name

Odorato erfunden und im Laufe der Zeit, entsprechend
Odorato invented and in the course of the time corresponding

den Fortschritten der Chemie, bedeutend vervollkommnet.
the progress of the chemistry significantly perfected

Das Instrument unserer Künstlerin war aus einer deutschen
The instrument of our artist was from a German

Fabrik und zeichnete sich durch seinen großen
factory and drew {zeichnete aus; distinguished} itself through by its large

Umfang an Gerüchen aus; es reichte von dem als unterste
size on smells ~~out~~ it reached from the as lowest
amount of

Duftstufe angenommenen dumpfen Keller- und
fragrance level adopted dull basement and

Modergeruche bis zum Zwiblozin, einem erst im Jahre
musty smells until to the zwiblozin a first in the year
only

2369 entdeckten äußerst zarten Odeur. Jeder Druck auf
2369 discovered extremely gentle smell Each press on

eine Taste öffnete einen entsprechenden Gasometer, und
a button opened a corresponding gasometer and

9

künstliche mechanische Vorrichtungen sorgten für die
artificial mechanical devices took care for the
of

Dämpfung, Ausbreitung und Zusammenwirkung der Düfte.
attenuation spread and interaction of the fragrances

Nachdem man die Musik auf einen solchen Höhepunkt
After one the music on a such climax

der Vervollkommnung gebracht hatte, dass das Ohr
of the perfection brought had that the ear

unmöglich mehr ertragen konnte, hatte man seine
impossible (any)more enduring could had one his

Aufmerksamkeit der so sehr vernachlässigten Nase
attention to the so very neglected nose

zugewandt. Die Feinheit des Geruchsorgans war freilich
turned to The fineness of the olfactory organ was indeed

bei der Menschheit in der Rückbildung begriffen; aber
by the mankind in the regression engaged but

warum sollte man diese nicht steuern können? Kein
why should one this not to direct be able No

anderer Sinn wirkt gleich lebhaft auf unsere
other sense works immediately lively on our

Ideenassoziation wie der des Geruchs; es lag nahe, ihn
association of ideas as that of the smell it lay close him
it

künstlerisch dazu zu verwerten, bestimmte Vorstellungen
artistically there-to to utilize certain imaginations

und Empfindungen in uns hervorzurufen. Man studierte die
and sensations in us to evoke One studied the

10

Eigentümlichkeiten und Wirkungen der Gerüche, fand die
peculiarities and effects of the smells found the

Gesetze ihrer Harmonie und Disharmonie, anfänglich auf
laws of her harmony and disharmony initially on

empirischem, später auch auf theoretischem Wege, die
empirical later also on theoretical way the
in a

Chemie stellte immer wohlfeiler die notwendigen
chemistry set always cheaper the necessary
{stellte her; created}

Aromen her, und nachdem das Ododion erst als Kuriosum
flavors away and after the Ododion first as curiosity

gezeigt und auf Rundreisen durch die Städte von aller
shown (was) and on round trips through the cities of all
tours

Welt angestaunt worden war, bürgerte es sich bald in
(the) world marveled at become was naturalized it itself soon in

den Familien, im Privatkreise ein.
the families in the private circles in

Die größten Duftmeister, zuerst Naso Odorato, dann
The greatest fragrance master first Naso Odorato then

Stinkerling, Frau Schnüffler, Riechmann, Aromasias Eltern
Stinkerling Mrs. Sniffler Smellman Aromasias parents

selbst, Herr Duftemann und Frau Ozodes, eine Griechin,
themselves Mr. Fragrantman and Mrs. Ozodes a Greek lady

leisteten Ododionpiecen, welche den Tonwerken der
accomplished Ododione pieces which the tone works of the

größten Musiker dreist an die Seite gestellt werden
great musician brazen on the side set become

konnten, und bald war das Ododion, das namentlich in
could and soon was the Ododion that especially in

seiner Verbindung mit der menschlichen Stimme hinreißend
its connection with the human voice adorable

wirkte, so in allen Häusern eingebürgert wie vor fünf
worked so in all houses naturalized as before five
earlier

Jahrhunderten das Klavier. Töchter und Söhne
centuries the (upright) piano Daughters and sons

räucherten in ihren Mußestunden darauf herum, und die
smoked in her leisure hours thereupon around and the

Nachbarn klagten und jammerten über die Stümperei, die
neighbors complained and whined over the bungling the

Geruchsüberladung und Nasenmarter gerade so, wie man
odor overload and nasal torture just so as one

früher über das Flügelspiel und die Ohrenquälerei
before over the wing-play and the ear torture
grand piano play

herzog.
drew away
complained

Aromasia Duftemann Ozodes aber war eine Künstlerin
Aromasia Fragrantman Ozodes however was an artist

im wahren Sinne des Worts. Ihre Duftakkorde
in the true sense of the words Her fragrance chords

umstrickten die Seele mit Allgewalt. Springauf, Flieder und
knitted the soul with omnipotent jump up lilac and

Rosen führten die Träume in die holde Zeit des Sommers
roses led the dreams in the fair time of the Summer

und der jungen Liebe; aber allmählich verschwimmen diese
and the young love but gradually blurred these

Düfte, wir glauben vor verwelkten Blumen zu stehen,
fragrances we believe before withered flowers to stand

und ein Gemisch von Jasmin und Schnittlauch durchzieht
and a mixture of jasmine and chives runs through

das Gemüt mit unendlicher Wehmut. Und nun aus der
the mind with unending melancholy And now from the

Ferne, durch diese Wehmut hindurch, riechen wir den
distance through this melancholy through smell we the

Hohn, den Leichtsinn des Treulosen im Dufte des
mock the carelessness of the unfaithful in the scent of the

Weines; mehr und mehr umhüllen uns Alkoholdämpfe –
wine more and more envelop us alcohol vapors –

da, wie ein Aufschrei des Entsetzens, ein
there as a (surprised) scream of the dismay a

Missgeruch! Pulver ist es, dann dunkle Grabesluft... Noch
bad smell Powder is it then dark grave air Still

einmal im unendlichen Schmerz erheben sich die
once in the infinite pain raise itself the

Duftakkorde, dann verduften sie in stiller Resignation...
fragrance chords then evaporate they in more quiet resignation

13

Aromasia ließ die Hand sinken. Da fühlte sie dieselbe
Aromasia let the hand sink There felt she the same

ergriffen und mit heißen Küssen bedeckt.
grasped and with hot kisses covered

Magnet Reimert-Oberton war unbemerkt zum Fenster herein
Magnet Rhymer-Overtone was unnoticed to the window inside

luftvelozipediert und zu ihren Füßen niedergesunken. Noch
air-bicycled and to her feet sunk down Still

bebte seine Seele im Nachgefühl des Spieles Aromasias.
shook his soul in the afterfeeling of the play of Aromasia

Magnet führte wie alle Leute einen Doppelnamen. Der
Magnet carried as all people a double name The

rechtlichen Gleichstellung der Frauen gemäß behielten
legal equality of the women according to kept

die Kinder sowohl den Namen der Mutter als den des
the children both the name of the mother as that of the

Vaters; verheirateten sie sich, so ließen die Töchter
father married they themselves so let the daughters

den Namen des Vaters, die Söhne den der Mutter fort
the name of the father the sons that of the mother away

und nahmen dafür den des Gemahls hinzu.
and took therefore that of the spouse there-to
added

14

Reimert-Oberton war ebenfalls Künstler, und zwar Dichter.
Rhymer-Overtone was likewise artist and indeed poet

Nach unseren Begriffen würde man ihn als einen
After our understanding would one him as an

unerträglichen Realisten bezeichnen, dem damaligen Zeitalter
intolerable realist describe the at that time age

aber galt er nicht nur als ein übermäßiger Idealist,
however was seen he not only as an excessive idealist

sondern auch als weichlicher Romantiker. Denn er stand
but also as soft romantic Then he stood
Because

noch auf dem Standpunkte der Dichter des
still on the viewpoints of the poets of the

dreiundzwanzigsten Jahrhunderts, welche sich gern in das
twenty-third century which itself gladly in the

Zeitalter des Dampfes zurückträumten, in jene Tage, als
age of the steam dreamed back in that one days as

die Menschen noch gezwungen waren, zu den Bergen
the people still compelled were to the mountains

aufzusehen. Er verzweifelte an der Macht der Poesie in
to look up He despaired at the power of the poetry in

einem Jahrhundert, in welchem man den rechnenden
a century in which one the arithmetic

Verstand vergötterte, und pries die Zeit des
mind idolized and praised the time of the

Neumittelalters glücklich, in welcher es nicht darauf
new middle ages happily in which it not thereupon

ankam, an ein heiliges Wunder zu glauben und mit
arrived to a holy miracle to believe and with
depended

Klopfgeistern zu verkehren. Eine Neuerung jedoch hatte er
poltergeists to associate One innovation however had he

versucht, welche ein Verdienst um die Literatur bildete,
tried which a merit for the literature formed

nämlich die Einführung der begrifflich strengen
namely the introduction of the conceptual severe

wissenschaftlichen und technischen Bezeichnungen der
scientific and technical designations of the

Vorgänge in die Poesie an Stelle der auf einer veralteten
operations in the poetry on spot of the on an outdated
in stead

Anschauung beruhenden so genannten poetischen. Übrigens
view based so mentioned poetic one By the way

dichtete er meist deutsch und verfasste nur die
wrote he most of time German and wrote only the

Grunzuletts in der Universalsprache.
greentreats in the universal language

»O große Aromasia«, rief er jetzt, »des
Oh great Aromasia « called he now of

vierundzwanzigsten Jahrhunderts erhabenste Ododistin! Ihnen
twenty-fourth century most sublime Ododist You

gehört der Schwingungszustand meiner Gehirnzellen, ihnen
belongs the vibrational state of my brain cells (for) you

bebt jede Nervenfaser meines Rückenmarks! Wie die Flur
trembles each nerve fiber of my spinal cord As the hall

den durch die mit Wasserdämpfen gesättigte Morgenluft
the through the with steam saturated morning air

stark absorbierten Sonnenstrahlen entgegenseufzt, so zittern
strong absorbed sunbeams towards sighs so tremble

nach den Düften ihres Ododions die zarten Häute meiner
to the smell of you Ododions the gentle skins of my

Nase!«
nose

»Magnet«, erwiderte Aromasia, mit dem Finger drohend,
Magnet answered Aromasia with the finger menacing

»seien Sie nicht unartig! Sie vergessen wieder, was wir
Be you not naughty You forget again what we

ausgemacht haben – Ihre Anbetung ist gestattet, aber in
decided have – your worship is allowed but in

geziemenden Grenzen. Sie verdienten wirklich, dass Ihnen
befitting limits You earned really that you

mein Bräutigam einen Regenguss über den Hals schickte.
my bridegroom a downpour over the neck sent

Ich will Oxygen darum bitten!«
I want Oxygen therefore ask

»Grausame! Ich fürchte keine Kondensation – die lebendige
Cruel one I fear no condensation – the lively

Kraft meines heißen Blutes wird die Wassermolekel
strength of my hot blood will the water molecule

auseinandertreiben.«
disperse

»Warten wir das ab! Übrigens wissen Sie selbst, wie sehr
Await / we / that / off / By the way / know / you / yourself / how / much
Let's await that

Sie übertreiben. Ihre Schmeicheleien müssen mir wie Spott
you / exaggerate / you / flatteries / must / me / as / ridicule

klingen, denn ich kenne zu gut meine schwachen Kräfte,
sound / then / I / know / too / well / my / weak / forces
because

welche die Ideale meiner Nase nicht erreichen. Wo
which / the / ideal / of my / nose / not / reach / Where

bleibt die Gedankentiefe eines Riechmann in meinem
remains / the / depth of thought / of a / Smellman / in / my

Gedüftel. Riechen Aromasia sagte: »Räuchen Sie.« Man
smellery / Smell / Aromasia / said / Smoke / you / One

hatte zur Unterscheidung vom Intransitivum »riechen«
had / to the / distinction / from the / intransitivum / smell

das Transitivum »räuchen« gebildet und sagte: Die Rose
the / transitivum / smoke / built / and / said / The / rose

riecht, roch, hat gerochen; der Mensch räucht, räuchte,
smells / smelled / has / smelled / the / human / smokes / smoked

hat geräucht. Leider müssen wir noch beim Alten
has / smoked / Unfortunately / must / we / still / at the / old

bleiben. Seh hier diesen einfachen Übergang vom
stay / See / here / this / simple / crossing / from the

aromatischen Drei-Duft durch den halben Mollgeruch in
aromatic / three-scented / through / the / half / foul smell / in

die Schlussozodie. Was liegt nicht alles in diesem
the / final ozodie / What / lies / not / everything / in / this

18

einfachen Zuge! Kraft, Todesmut, Stärke, Stiergebrüll, die
simple moves force death courage strength bull roar the

ganze Geschichte der Erfindung des elektromotorischen
whole story of the invention of the electromotive

Schnellwagens, Menschengröße, Gewitter, Winzertanz und
express car human size thunderstorm winemaker dance and

sogar die Elemente der Kometbahn von
even the elements of the comet orbit from

neunzehnhundertachzig. Das kann aber auch nur ein
nineteen eighty That can however also only a

Richard Riechmann.«
Richard Smellman

»Sie sind zu bescheiden. Haben doch auch Sie schon die
You are too modest have indeed also you already the

Überwindung des Materialismus durch den Kritizismus und
overcoming of the materialism through the criticism and

die Vollendung des Nikaragua-Kanals auf dem Ododion
the completion of the nicaragua channel on the Ododion

dargestellt.«
shown

»Es sind schwache Versuche! O Magnet, arm wird uns
It are weak attempts Oh Magnet, poor will us
They

der Meister erstehen, welcher das Geruchsdrama der
the master arise which the olfactory drama of the

Zukunft schafft! Riechmann? Ihm mangelt die gestaltende
future creates Smellman Him lacks the creative

19

Kraft der Sprache - ach, Magnet, warum sind Sie kein
strength of the language - Oh Magnet why are you no

Duftkünstler?«
fragrance artist

»Weil ich leider nur ein Dichter bin, aber ein
Because I unfortunately only a poet am but a

schlechter. Doch nicht in der Zukunft dürfen Sie unsere
bad (one) Indeed not in the future may you our

Ideale suchen, greifen Sie zurück in die Vergangenheit.«
ideal search grasp you back in the past

»Ich bitte Sie, Shakespeare, Goethe...«
I ask you Shakespeare Goethe

»Viel zu veraltet, nein - aber Anton Feuerhase und sein
Much to outdated no - but Anton Firebunny and his

Trauerspiel ›Die letzte Lokomotive‹! Das ist Poesie! Denken
tragedy The last locomotive That is poetry Think

Sie an die Schlussszene mit der Musik von Brummer -
you on the final scene with the music from Grumbler -

die Ododionbegleitung ist, glaub' ich, von Stinkerling -,
the Ododion accompaniment is believe I of Stinkerling -,

wie der Kessel platzt, der unselige Lokomotivführer, der
as the boiler bursts the unfortunate engine driver who

im Zwiespalt der Pflichten zwischen der Rettung des
in the conflict of the duties between the rescue of the

Publikums und des Eigentums der Bahnverwaltung
audience and of the property of the railway administration

untergeht, in die Luft geschleudert, mitten zwischen
goes down in the air hurled middle between
in the middle of

den Trümmern, nachdem er schon die Kinnlade und ein
the ruins after he already the jaw and a

Bein verloren, hinunterdonnert zu den Wagons.
leg lost thunders down to the wagons

Vergebens, Dampf, dass du den Atem hemmst!
In vain Steam that you the breath inhibit

Der Eilzug stürzt! Ade, mein Bein! Bremst! Bremst!
The express train crashes Goodbye my leg Brake Brake

Wenn dann der Vorhang fällt und die Musik das Geräusch
When then the curtain falls and the music the sound

der Bremsen noch nachtönen lässt, dann erst fühlt man,
of the brake still aftertone lets then first feels one
sound out

was die Dichtkunst vermag. Und mir gelingt es nicht
what the poetry might And me succeeds it not
can do

einmal, ein armseliges Grunzulett ins Deutsche zu
once a poor greentreat in the German to

übertragen.«
transfer

»Aber es gelingt Ihnen, so manches Gemüt zu erheben
But it succeeds you so much mind to raise

über die Gewöhnlichkeit des Lebens und sich
over the ordinaryness of the life and yourself

unabhängig zu fühlen vom verwirrenden Urteil der
independent to feel from the confusing judgement of the

Menge. Und das ist es, was ich an unserer Kunst
Mass(es) And that is it what I on of our art

preise.«
prize

»Nicht alle werden es Ihnen zugeben. Die Partei,
Not all will it you admit The political party

welche sich den Namen der ›Nüchternen‹ gegeben hat,
which himself the name the Sober ones given has

behauptet, dass nur durch die Bildung des Verstandes ein
claimed that only through the education of the mind a

Fortschritt der Menschheit möglich sei; dass die
progress of the mankind possible be is that the

intellektuelle Entwicklung, wie sie die Emanzipation von
intellectual development as she the emancipation from

der Naturgewalt geleistet habe, auch allein
the natural force accomplished has also alone

im Stande sei, von den Leidenschaften zu befreien
in the stand be (itself) from the passions to to free
is able

und die Menschheit ihrer sittlichen Vollendung und mehr
and the mankind her moral completion and more

entgegenzuführen; ja, dass wir den Errungenschaften der
to lead towards yes that we the achievements of the

Wissenschaften allein den hohen Kulturzustand der
sciences alone the high state of culture of the

22

Gegenwart	in	ethischer	Beziehung	verdanken,	unsere
present (time)	in	ethical	relationship	owe	our

Toleranz,	unsere	Milde,	unsere	Reinheit	der	Gesinnung.«
tolerance	our	mildness	our	purity	of the	attitude

»Magnet,	Sie	erinnern	mich	zur	Unzeit	an	diesen
Magnet	you	remind	me	at the	bad time	on	this

unseligen	Parteistreit,	der	so	tief	in	die	Verhältnisse
unfortunate	party dispute	which	so	deep	in	the	conditions

unseres	Lebens	eingreift.	Sie	wissen,	dass	hier	der	einzige
(of) our	life	intervenes	You	know	that	here	the	only

Punkt	liegt,	der	mich	von	Oxygen	trennt,	dass	hier	allein
point	lies	the	me	from	Oxygen	separates	that	here	alone

unsere	Meinungen	auseinander	gehen.	Und	doch	kann
our	opinions	out (of) each other apart	go lie	And	indeed	can

ich	nicht	anders,	wie	lieb	ich	meinen	Bräutigam	habe
I	not	otherwise	how(ever)	dear	I	my	bridegroom	have

–	es	ist	meine	heiligste	Überzeugung,	dass	allein	dem
–	it	is	my	most sacred	conviction	that	alone	the

Einflusse	der	Künste,	insbesondere	der	Ododistik,	auf	den
influences	of the	arts	in particular	the	Ododistics	on	the

Menschen	die	Erhebung	der	Sittlichkeit	und	die	Förderung
people	the	lifting	of the	morality	and	the	advancement

der	Zivilisation	zugeschrieben	werden	kann:	Nur	zu	oft
of the	civilization	attributed to	become	can	Only	too	often

23

macht diese Meinungsverschiedenheit uns bittere Stunden,
makes / gives — this — disagreement — us — bitter — hours

und ich fürchte...«
and — I — fear

»Nicht doch Aromasia! Sie sagten selbst so oft, dass
Not however / But that's not true — Aromasia — You — said — yourself — so — often — that

bei der Gewohnheit unserer Zeit, jegliches Urteil
according to — the — habits — of our — time — any — judgement

gelten zu lassen und die Sache von der Person zu
be valid — to — let / to allow — and — the — thing — from — the — person — to

trennen, eine persönliche Anfeindung aus einem Streite
separate — a — personal — hostility — from — an — argument

der Anschauungen überhaupt nicht mehr entstehen
about the — (world) views — at all — not — (any)more — arise

könne. Wie mögen Sie solche Befürchtungen durch die aus
could — How — may / can — you — such — fears — through — the — from

den Bewegungen ihrer Mundhöhle resultierenden
the — movements — of your — oral cavity — resulting

Schallwellen ausdrücken?«
sound waves — express

»Weil ich gar nicht so sicher bin, dass unser Zeitalter
Because — I — at all — not — so — sure — am — that — our — age

wirklich auf einer so gepriesenen Höhe objektiver
really — on — a — such — praised — height — of objective

Betrachtung steht. Wäre es nur ein rein theoretischer
consideration stands Were it only a purely theoretical

Streit, um den es sich handelte, so wollte ich mich
conflict about which it itself deals so would I myself

beruhigen. Aber wie oft auch die Nüchternen dies
calm down But how often also the sober ones this

behaupten mögen, es ist nicht wahr. Hier liegt ein
claim may it is not true Here lies a

Gegensatz vor, der tief in der Natur des Menschen
contrast before (us) which deep in the nature of the people

begründet ist, der immer bestanden hat und bestehen
justified is which always existed has and exist

wird und sich gegenwärtig nur in dieser Form ausspricht.
will and itself currently only in this form pronounces

Wir sind nicht mehr im Stande, in tödliche Feindschaft
We are not (any)more in the stand in deadly enmity
                                     able

zu geraten, weil einige religiöse Dogmen bei dem einen
to become because some religious dogmen at the one

anders lauten als beim Nachbar, aber der unauslöschliche
different sounds as at the neighbor but the indelible

Kampf entgegengesetzter Ideale äußert sich dafür im
fight of opposite ideals expresses itself therefore in the

Parteihader der ›Nüchternen‹ und der ›Innigen‹. Die
party arena of the sober ones and the intimate ones Those
                                                 emotional ones

Namen sind unglücklich genug gewählt. Die Nüchternen
name are unfortunately enough chosen The sober ones

25

sind die allerschlimmsten Fanatiker; wenn sie sich auf
are the worst fanatics when they themselves on

die ›nüchterne Überlegung‹ berufen, so lügen sie. Ihre
the sober consideration appeal so lie they Their

innerste Gemütsanlage ist eben fremd und abgeneigt
innermost mood system is as strange and averse

den warmen Empfindungen einer ideal fühlenden Seele,
from the warm sensations of an ideal sentient soul

die das Leben erfasst wie es sein soll, und nicht
who ~~the~~ life grasps as it be should and not

zergliedert, wie es ist.«
dissected as it is

»Seien Sie nicht so böse, Aromasia«, tröstete Magnet. »Bei
Be you not so angry Aromasia comforted Magnet By

diesen Leuten sind nun einmal die Zentralorgane der
these people are now once the central organs of the
in any case

Geruchsempfindungen, das Subiculum des Ammonshorns
olfactory sensations the subiculum of the ammonshorns
{nasal biology}

oder die Spitze der ›hakenförmigen‹ Windungen schlecht
or the tip of the hook-shaped turns bad

entwickelt. Ihr Gehirn ist einer feinen Duftempfindung
developed Their brain is for a delicate fragrance sensation

nicht zugänglich, und sie werden eine Aromasia nie
not accessible and they will an Aromasia never

verstehen.«
understand

26

»Und Oxygen?«
And Oxygen

Magnet schwieg. Sanft irrten Aromasias Finger über die
Magnet was silent Gently roamed Aromasia's fingers over the

Tasten, die zarte Wohlgerüche ausströmten.
keys which delicate fragrances emanated

Eine Luftdroschke schwirrte vor das Fenster, Oxygen
An airboat whirred before the window Oxygen

führte sie. Er stellte die Schraube des Apparates
led her He set the screw of the machine
it propellor

horizontal, so dass die Drehung derselben den Wagen nur
horizontal so that the rotation of the same the cart only
of it

schwebend erhielt, ohne ihn fortzutreiben, befestigte das
floating kept without it to continue fortified the

Fahrzeug am Fenster und trat mit freundlichem Gruß
vehicle at the window and stepped with friendly greeting

ins Zimmer.
in the room

Aromasia eilte ihm entgegen und begrüßte ihn herzlich.
Aromasia hurried him towards and greeted him cordially

Ihr folgte Magnet. Oxygen näherte sich, Aromasia an
Her followed Magnet Oxygen approached himself Aromasia by

27

der Hand führend, dem Fenster und blickte in ein dort
the hand leading to the window and looked in a there

aufgestelltes Mikroskop.
set up microscope

»Allerliebst«, sagte er, »ich gratuliere, Aromasia. Selten
Dearest said he I congratulate Aromasia Rarely

habe ich einen so vorzüglichen Urschleim gesehen wie
have I a such excellent ancient slime seen as

diesen hier. Prächtig gelungen.«
this here Wonderfully succeeded

»Dir zu Liebe Oxygen«, erwiderte seine Braut. »Ich weiß,
You for dear Oxygen answered his bride I know

wie sehr du dich freust, wenn ich mich deiner
how much you yourself becomes happy when I myself your

kleinen Lieblinge annehme. So habe ich manche Stunde
small darlings accept So have I many hours

vor dem Mikroskop gesessen und der Zellbildung
before the microscope sat and the cell formation

zugesehen.«
watched

Es war damals Mode, den so genannten Urschleim, das
It was at that time fashion the so mentioned ancient slime the

niedrigste organische Gebilde, aus anorganischen Stoffen zu
lowest organic formation from inorganic fabrics to

ziehen. Professor Selberzelle hatte den Triumph gehabt, die
pull Professor Selfcell had the triumph had the
procreate

28

erste zweifellose Urzeugung zu beobachten, und statt
first undoubtedly Ancient-procreation to observe and instead

mit Papageien oder Schoßhündchen spielten Damen und
with parrots or lapdog played ladies and

Herren in ihren Mußestunden jetzt unter dem Mikroskop
gentlemen in their leisure hours now under the microscope

mit den zarten Urschleimtypen.
with the gentle primitive slime types

»Du bist später als gewöhnlich gekommen«, fuhr Aromasia
You are later as usually come carried Aromasia

fort. »Du hattest viel zu tun?«
forth You had much to do

»Leider, ich bin sehr mit Bestellungen überhäuft, das
Unfortunately I am much with orders over-heaped the

Wetter ist bei uns ausnahmsweise trocken, und ich habe
weather is at us exceptionally dry and I have

alle Mühe, Wasser genug zu schaffen. Und heute hatte ich
all trouble water enough to create And today had I

besonders viel zu besorgen, denn ich wollte mich für
particularly much to deliver then I wanted myself for

morgen frei machen. Ich habe dir nämlich einen Vorschlag
tomorrow free make I have you namely a proposal

mitzuteilen – ich denke, Magnet, du wirst auch dabei
with-to-share – I think Magnet you will also there-by
to tell

sein?«
be

29

Nun entwickelte Oxygen seine Idee.
Now developed Oxygen his idea

Oxygen Warm-Blasius war seines Zeichens nichts Geringeres
Oxygen Warm-Blasius was his mark's nothing less

als Wetterfabrikant; das heißt, er war Besitzer eines
as weather manufacturer that is called he was owner of a
that is

großen Etablissements, welches Apparate herstellte und
large establishment which machines manufactured and

verlieh, um Veränderungen in der Atmosphäre künstlich
rented out for changes in the atmosphere artfully

hervorzurufen. Dies geschah durch chemische und
to evoke This happened through chemical and

physikalische Kräfte; da wurden Dämpfe entwickelt, große
physical forces there became fumes developed great

Luftmassen erhitzt oder abgekühlt, obere Luftschichten in
air masses heated or cooled down upper air layers in

niedere Regionen gesogen, tiefere hinaufgepresst, Wolken
lower regions sucked lower pressed up clouds

gebildet und zerstreut. Oxygens Geschicklichkeit hatte sein
built and destroyed Oxygen's skill had his

Etablissement zu einem sehr beliebten gemacht.
establishment to a very popular one made

»Ich habe also für morgen meine Geschäfte bereits
I have thus for tomorrow my activities already

geordnet«, fuhr er jetzt fort, »um mit euch eine kleine
ordered drove he now away for with you a little
finished carried on

30

Partie für den ganzen Tag zu arrangieren. Es ist nämlich
party for the whole day to arrange It is namely

gerade morgen einer der so sehr seltenen Tage, an
just tomorrow one of the so very rare days on

denen die ganze nördliche Erdkugel heiteres Wetter besitzt,
which the whole northern globe cheerful weather possesses
gets

und wir können daher unsern Ausflug beliebig einrichten,
and we can there-from our excursion in any way arrange

ohne künstlicher Hilfe zu bedürfen oder irgendeine
without more artificial help to need or some

Störung befürchten zu müssen.«
disturbance to fear to have to

»Und wohin willst du?«, fragte Magnet.
and where-to want you asked Magnet

»Ich schlage vor, nach dem Niagarafall zu fahren.
I strike before to the Niagara fall(s) to drive
propose fly

Anfänglich dachte ich an die Nilquellen, aber dort
Initially thought I on the Sources of the Nile but there
of

waren wir erst im Winter, und in den Tropen ist auch
were we first in the winter and in the tropics is also

der Aufenthalt in gegenwärtiger Jahreszeit nicht gerade
the delay in more current season not very

angenehm.
pleasant

»Zum Niagara«, rief Aromasia, »das hast du gut
To the Niagara called Aromasia that have you good

ausgedacht, Oxy! Aber da müssen wir wohl zeitig
made up Oxy But there must we well in time
                          then

hinaus?«
away-out
leave

»Wenn wir um sechs Uhr abfahren, so haben wir übrig
if we around six hours off-drive so have we enough
        at   depart

Zeit, auch ohne unsere Maschine zu sehr anzustrengen.
time also without our machine to much to strain

Selbst wenn wir uns vier Stunden -Zur Bequemlichkeit
Even when we ourselves four hours for the convenience

für den Leser des 19. Jahrhunderts (wir begnügen
for the reader of the 19th century we satisfy
of

uns, für diesen zu schreiben) sind hier solche Stunden
ourselves for this one to write are here such hours

genommen, von denen 24 auf einen Tag gehen- am Fall
taken from which 24 on a day go at the falls

aufhalten, können wir um zehn Uhr abends wieder
up-hold can we for ten hour(s) in the evening again
stop over

zurück sein. Sechs Stunden brauchen wir zur Hinfahrt.
back be Six hours need we to the trip there

32

Ich würde aber vorschlagen, lieber schon um vier oder
I would however propose rather already around four or
at

ein halb fünf Uhr, gleichzeitig mit der Sonne,
one half five hour(s) at the same time with the sun

aufzubrechen. Da wir nach Westen fahren, können wir
to break up There we to (the) west drive can we
As go

unsere Geschwindigkeit so wählen, dass wir der
our speed so choose that we the

entgegengesetzten Drehung der Erde ganz genau das
opposite-set rotation of the earth completely exactly the

Gleichgewicht halten und sie für uns paralysieren. Wir
balance hold and her for us paralyze We
it freeze

genießen dann, den Blick zurückgewendet, das Schauspiel
enjoy then the glance turned back the spectacle

eines sechsstündigen Sonnenaufgangs, der sich auf dem
of a six hour (long) sunrise which itself on the

Atlantischen Ozean ganz prachtvoll macht.«
atlantic ocean completely magnificent makes

»Vor uns den Tag und hinter uns die Nacht«, zitierte
In front of us the day and behind us the night quoted

Magnet.
Magnet

33

»Eigentlich müsste es bei uns umgekehrt heißen«, meinte
Actually should it at us upside down be called thought

Oxygen, »aber wir müssen die Alten verbrauchen, wie sie
Oxygen but we must the old consume as they

sind.«
are

»Dieser Ausfall sei dir verziehen, teurer Oxygen«, rief
This sortie be you forgiven dear Oxygen called
exclamation

Magnet, »denn deine Idee ist wirklich brillant, grunzulettal!
Magnet because your idea is really brilliant greentreatish

Freilich kommen wir auf diese Weise auch schon nach
Indeed come we on this manner also already at
arrive

unserem Ziele, wenn es dort erst vier Uhr morgens
our target when it there only four hour(s) (in the) morning

ist.«
is

»Dafür, weiser Dichter, entgehen wir auch der Mittagshitze
For this wise poet escape we also the midday heat

auf dem Lande. Um acht oder neun Uhr brechen wir
on the land At eight or nine hour(s) break we

dann auf, sechs Stunden zurück, das heißt relativ zwölf
then up six hours back the is called relative twelve

Stunden, da wir jetzt der Sonne mit derselben
hours there we now the sun with the same

34

Geschwindigkeit entgegeneilen, als wir auf der Hinfahrt
speed   hurry up   as   we   on   the   there

vor ihr herflogen, und um acht Uhr nach mittlerer
before   her   flew here   and   for   guard   hour   to   middle

Berliner Zeit sind wir wieder zu Hause, also noch bei
donut   time   are   we   again   to   house   thus   still   at

Tageslicht.«
daylight

»Und für morgen bist du des Wetters ganz sicher?«,
And   for   tomorrow   are   you   of the   weather   completely   sure

fragte Aromasia.
asked   Aromasia

»Überzeuge dich selbst«, erwiderte Oxygen, indem er aus
Convince   you(r)   self   answered   Oxygen   while   he   from

seinem Wagen den Wetteratlas holte und den betreffenden
his   cart   the   weather atlas   got   and   the   concerned

Tag aufschlug.
day   upstruck
     opened

Im Wetteratlas findet sich auf ein halbes Jahr im
In the   weather atlas   finds   itself   on   a   half   year   in the

Voraus für jeden Tag der Zustand der Atmosphäre auf
advance   for   every   day   the   status   of the   atmosphere   on

der ganzen Erde angegeben. Bis auf die halbe Meile und
the   whole   Earth   specified   Up to   on   the   half   mile   and

die Viertelstunde bestimmte die Meteorologie die Witterung
the quarter of an hour decides the meteorology the weather
figures out

mit mathematischer Genauigkeit. Auf kolorierten Erdkarten
with mathematical accuracy On colored earth maps

in großem Maßstabe waren diese wissenschaftlichen
in great scale were this scientific

Ergebnisse verzeichnet, jedem Tage gehörte eine Karte.
results recorded each days belonged to a card

»Ihr seht«, fuhr Oxygen fort und blätterte in den Karten,
You see drove oxygen away and leafed in the cards
carried on

»Regenstreifen überall im Westen – nur morgen
Rain stripes everywhere in the west – only tomorrow

prachtvollstes Wetter. Also abgemacht?«
most magnificent weather Thus agreed

»Abgemacht! Vorbereitungen sind ja nicht nötig.«
Settled Preparations are yes not necessary
Agreed indeed

»Gut, so fahren wir morgen früh vier Uhr in meinem
Good so drive we tomorrow early (at) four hour(s) in my

neuen Motor.«
new engine

»Das muss ich gestehen«, fügte Aromasia hinzu, »dieses
That must I confess added Aromasia there-to this

Verdienst der Wissenschaft erkenne ich an, welches sie
merit of the science recognize I on which she

36

sich um unsere Garderoben erworben hat. Wie grässlich
herself for our closets acquired has How awful

muss es gewesen sein, als man von solchen Zufälligkeiten,
must it been be if one from such coincidences
have

wie es ein Regenguss, ein Windstoß scheinbar sind, in
as it a downpour a gust of wind apparently are in

allen seinen Bestimmungen abhängig war.«
all their provisions dependent were

»Nur von einem Naturzwange konnten wir uns
Only from a natural constraint could we ourselves

vorläufig nicht befreien«, sagte Oxygen lächelnd, »nämlich
for now not free said Oxygen smiling namely

vom Hunger. Und ich muss gestehen, es wäre mir
from the hunger And I must confess it would be to me

lieb, wenn...«
dear if

»Wir sind bereit«, rief Aromasia, indem sie einen
We are ready called Aromasia while she a

kräftigen Bratengeruch auf dem Ododion anschlug.
powerful smell of roast on the Ododion struck

Und die Gesellschaft bestieg den Luftmotor Oxygens, um
And the company mounted the air motor of Oxygen for

sich in das Speisehaus zu begeben.
themselves in the food house to issue
go

Im Pyramidenhotel
In the Pyramid hotel

Im — großen — Speisesaale — des — Pyramidenhotels — herrschte — ein
In the — large — dining room — of the — pyramid hotel — ruled / prevailed — a

reges — Leben. — Luftdroschken — fuhren — ab — und — zu; — an — den
lively / lively bustle — life — Air carriages — drove — off — and — on — on — the

Büfetts, — welche — sich — längs — der — Wände — hinzogen,
buffets — which — themselves — along — the — walls — stretched

drängten — sich — die — Geschäftsleute — und — die
pressed — themselves — the — business people — and — the

Durchreisenden, — im — Vorbeigehen — die
~~through~~ travelers — in the — passing — of the

Universal-Kraft-Extraktpillen — dieser — oder — jener — Speise
universal power extract pills — this — or — that — meal

einzunehmen, — welche — sie — in — den — Stand — setzten, — in
in to take — which — them — in — the — stand enabled — set — in

wenigen — Sekunden — eine — Mahlzeit — von — mehreren — Gängen — zu
few — seconds — a — meal — from — several — courses — to

genießen. — Diejenigen, — welche — mit — ihrer — Zeit — in — gleichem
enjoy — Those — which — with — their — time — in — equal

Maß — zu — sparen — nicht — nötig — hatten, — saßen — an — den
measure — to — spare — not — necessary — had — sat — on — the

geschmückten — Tafeln — in — der — Mitte — des — Saales. — An — jedem
decorated — tables — in — the — middle — of the — hall — On — each

Platze — befand — sich — eine — Anzahl — Knöpfe, — deren
place — found — itself — a — number — (of) buttons — of which

Aufschriften die Speisekarte darstellte, und ein Druck auf
(the) inscriptions the food-card represented and one press on
menu

dieselbe zauberte, dem »Tischlein, deck dich« gleich, die
the same conjured up the little table deck yourself similar the

verlangte Schüssel unter der Tischplatte hervor.
desired dish (from) under the tabletop forth

Die Verkehrsmittel des 24. Jahrhunderts ließen jedes Land
The means of transport of the 24. century let each country

seine Tribute darbringen. Dieses Schnabeltier hatte noch
its tribute offer This platypus had still

vorgestern in van Diemens Land die Ameisen in
the day before yesterday in van Diemens land the ants in

Schrecken versetzt; der Singschwanflügel, den Aromasia
fright set the Whooper-swan wing which Aromasia

eben zerlegte, war erst gestern in Nowaja-Semlja vom
just disassembled was first yesterday in Novaya-Zemlya from the
ate only by the

Schlage des elektrischen Jagdgewehrs gelähmt worden. Die
strike of the electrical hunting rifle paralyzed become The

Zeit der Reise schien keinen Einfluss mehr auf den
time of the journey seemed no influence (any)more on the

Verbrauch der Früchte zu üben. Auf dem unendlichen
consumption of the fruit to practice On the infinite
have

Streifen, welcher in der Mitte des Tisches alle auf ihm
line which in the middle of the table all on him

niedergestellten Tafelzierden in steter Bewegung an den
put down table decorations in always movement on the

Gästen vorüberführte, prangten die schönsten ungarischen
guests passed emblazoned the most beautiful Hungarian

Trauben neben deutschen Erdbeeren, Apfelsinen,
grapes beside German strawberries oranges

vor einer Stunde in Sardinien vom Baume gepflückt,
before an hour in Sardinia from the tree picked
an hour ago

daneben fleischige Acaju-Nüsse aus Brasilien und in kleinen
there next meaty cashews from Brazil and in small

Kristallschalen frische Kokosmilch von den Nikobaren.
crystal bowls fresh coconut milk from the Nicobars (islands)

Gemischt aus allen Zonen, wie das Menü, waren auch die
Mixed from all zones like the menu were also the

Scharen der Speisenden. Denn die ganze Menschheit war
flocks of the diners Then the whole mankind was
all of

in einem ewigen Wandern und Strömen durcheinander
in an eternal roaming and flowing through-each other
mingling

begriffen. Ob dies gleich mehr an den Büfetts,
engaged Whether this immediately more on the buffets
rather

weniger an den Tafeln hervortrat, wo fast nur die
less on the tables emerged where almost only the

einheimischen Familien speisten, war doch auch hier der
native families dined was indeed also here the

kosmopolitische Zug des Jahrhunderts wohl zu merken.
cosmopolitan train of the century well to notice

Mit Ausnahme des allerreichsten Teiles der Bevölkerung,
With exception of the very richest part of the population

welcher es durchsetzen konnte, seinen eigenen Tisch zu
which it push through could their own table to

haben, war jeder darauf angewiesen, in den öffentlichen
have was each thereupon reliant in the public

Garküchen zu speisen. Denn mit der Vermehrung der
food stalls to eat Then with the increase of the
                        Because

Bevölkerung konnte die Produktion der Nahrungsmittel nur
population could the production of the means of feeding only
                                              food

mühsam Schritt halten, und die Verteuerung der
tediously step hold and the getting more expensive of the

Rohstoffe ließ sich nur dadurch ausgleichen, dass die
raw materials let itself only there-through compensate that the
                              through that

Kosten der Zubereitung durch die Speisegenossenschaften
costs the preparation through the food cooperatives

auf ein Minimum reduziert wurden. Die Güte und
on a minimum reduced became The quality and

Reichhaltigkeit der Gerichte konnte dadurch natürlich
richness of the dishes could there-through of course
                                   through that

nur gewinnen, leider aber verlor der
only win unfortunately however lost the

Familienzusammenhang und die Poesie des Hauses umso
family context and the poetry of the house all the

41

mehr durch die nivellierende Öffentlichkeit. Schwarzseher
more through the leveling public nature (of it) Doomlookers / Doomsayers

prophezeiten wohl schon den Untergang der Sitte und
prophesied well already the going down / doom of the habits and

Kultur; aber das ist allezeit geschehen, und jeder
culture but that is / has all the time happened and each

Vorurteilsfreie musste eingestehen, dass trotz manch
unprejudiced (person) had to admit that despite many

wunderlicher Gegensätze zu gleicher Höhe sittlicher Freiheit
whimsical opposites to similar height (of) moral freedom

und allgemeinen Glücks die Menschheit sich noch nie
and general happiness the mankind itself still never

erhoben hatte.
arisen had

Mit Eifer blickte man nach den großen Tafeln der
With zeal looked one at the large panel of the

Drucktelegrafen im Hintergrund des Saales, auf welchen
print telegraph in the background of the hall on which

die mannigfaltigen Nachrichten aus allen Weltgegenden
the varied new articles from all regions of the world

sofort selbsttätig in stenografischer Schrift sich
immediately automatically in stenographic writing themselves

verzeichneten. Das Tagesgespräch bildete der Konflikt
recorded / showed The daily conversation formed the conflict

zwischen den Vereinigten Staaten und dem chinesischen
between the United States and the Chinese

Kaiserreich, welches ihnen das Durchflugsrecht zu wehren
empire which them the right of flight to defend

versuchte. Doch wollte man an einen Krieg nicht glauben,
tried Indeed wanted one on/in a war not believe

da man sich von der Hoffnung nicht trennen konnte,
there one oneself from the hope not separate could

der so genannte Eisenbahnkrieg zwischen Russland und
the so called railroad war between Russia and

China im Jahre 2005 möge der letzte Krieg der
China in the year 2005 may the last war of the

zivilisierten Erde gewesen sein. Die Chinesen waren durch
civilized Earth been be/have The Chinese were through

denselben gezwungen worden, ihr Land dem europäischen
the same compelled become their land the european

Eisenbahnverkehr zu eröffnen; aber in demselben Jahr, in
rail transport to open but in the same year in

welchem die mittelasiatische Pazifik-Bahn vollendet war,
which the central asian pacific railroad accomplished was

erlitt das Verkehrswesen durch die Erfindung des
suffered the transportation through the invention of the

Luftmotors eine derartige Umwälzung, dass die russischen
air motor a such turn around change that the Russian

Errungenschaften bald ihre Bedeutung verloren.
achievements soon their meaning lost

Auch an Aromasias Tische sprach man von den politischen
Also at Aromasia's table spoke one from the political

Verhältnissen, und es war natürlich, dass man sich zu
conditions and it was of course that one themselves to

einem Vergleiche mit den Zuständen vor dem
a comparison with the situations before the
conditions

Eisenbahnkriege geführt fand. Magnet konnte unmöglich
railroad wars carried found Magnet could impossibly

von seiner Lieblingsepoche reden hören, ohne sich mit
from his favorite epoch talk hear without himself with

einer Lobrede auf dieselbe am Gespräch zu beteiligen;
a eulogy on the same at the conversation to participate

und Oxygen wurde dadurch unwillkürlich herausgefordert,
and Oxygen became there-through involuntarily challenged
through that

die Gegenwart der Vergangenheit gegenüber in Schutz zu
the presence to the past opposite in protection to

nehmen.
take

»Vor allen Dingen können Sie doch nicht leugnen«, sagte
Before all things can you indeed not deny said

er zu Magnet, »dass in allem, was den Komfort des
he to Magnet that in everything what the comfort of the

Lebens und das physische Wohlbefinden der Menschheit –
life and the physical wellbeing of the mankind –

ohne Bevorzugung der Einzelnen – anbetrifft, unsere Zeit
without preference of the individual – concerns our time

alle früheren Epochen ungemein überragt. Wie wäre es
all earlier/old epochs ungeneric/immensely towers over How would be/would have it

möglich gewesen, dass alle Schichten der Bevölkerung in
possible been that all layers of the population in

gleichem Maße an den Vorteilen der Kultur partizipierten,
equal measure to the benefits of the culture participated

hätte nicht der Fortschritt der Wissenschaften die
had not the progress of the sciences the

Naturkräfte in so reichem Masse dienstbar gemacht und
natural forces / forces of nature in such (a) rich quantity subservient made and

ihnen den Mechanismus der Arbeit so ausschließlich
(to) them the mechanism of the work so exclusively

aufgebürdet, dass ein jeder ein menschenwürdiges Dasein
burdened up / charged that one each / each one a decent there-be / existence

zu führen vermag? Wie wäre es möglich gewesen, die
to lead may As would be / would have it possible been the

blutigen Revolutionen der verschiedenen Stände
bloody revolutions of the different stands / classes

gegeneinander zu vermeiden, wäre nicht überall die
to each other to avoid would be / would have not everywhere the

Erkenntnis eingedrungen, dass nur im friedlichen
understanding penetrated that only in the peaceful

45

Zusammenwirken aller Berufskreise der Ausgleich jener
together-working all professional groups the compensation of that
cooperation equalization

Unterschiede zu ermöglichen ist, welcher durch die
difference to enable is which through the
because of

individuelle Verschiedenheit der menschlichen Natur immer
individual diversity of the human nature always

aufs Neue gesetzt wird. Nur die Einsicht in den
on the new set will only the insight in the
again

Zusammenhang der geschichtlichen Entwicklung der
context of the historical development of the

Gesellschaft und das Ineinandergreifen der
society and the interlocking of the

Wirkungssphären kann den ungünstiger Situierten
spheres of impact can the less favorable situated
blessed

veranlassen, sich mit dem zufriedenzugeben, was er
induce themselves with that to satisfy what he

seiner Kraft nach zu leisten vermag; und dieselbe
from his strength after to succeed may and the same
according to his strength

Einsicht allein kann den Reichen und Mächtigen zwingen,
insight alone can the rich and mighty force

seine Obermacht nicht zu missbrauchen und aus freien
their supreme power not to abuse and from free

Stücken bei einer gewissen Grenze des Erwerbes sich
pieces at a certain limit of the acquisition themselves
will

46

zu bescheiden, so dass die Vorteile der modernen
to modest limit / so / that / the / benefits / of the / modern

Industrie und Technik wirklich der Gesamtheit zugute
industry / and / technology / really / the / entirety / benefit

kommen. Und...«
come / And

»Erlaube«, unterbrach ihn Magnet, »die Tatsache muss ich
Allow (me) / interrupted / him / Magnet / that / fact / must / I

zwar anerkennen, dass wir die Klippe der sozialen Frage
indeed / recognize / that / we / the / cliff / of the / social / question

in ihrer krassen Form nach den großen Kämpfen des
in / her / blatant / form / after / the / large / struggles / of the

zwanzigsten Jahrhunderts glücklich umschifft haben.
twentieth / century / happily / circumnavigated / have

Deiner Hervorhebung der Ursache, die du in der
Your / highlighting / of the / root cause / that / you / in / the

vernunftgemäßen Überlegung finden willst, kann ich aber
reasonable / consideration / find / want / can / I / however

in nur sehr geringem Maße zustimmen. All diese Einsicht,
in / only / very / little / measure amount / agree to / All / this / insight

alle theoretische Erkenntnis ist machtlos gegenüber der
all / theoretical / understanding / is / powerless / opposite / the

Gewalt des Erhaltungstriebes im Kampfe ums Dasein,
force / of the / conservation drive / in the / fight / for the / existence

gegenüber der aufgestachelten Lust an Besitz und
against / the / incited / desire / for / possession / and

47

Genuss und der Leidenschaft des Moments. Diese Kräfte
pleasure and the passion of the moment These forces

konnten nur gebändigt werden durch eine Kraft des
could only subdued become through a strength of the

Gemütes, welche unsern Willen in gleich mächtiger Weise
mood which our will in equal powerful manner
soul

zu erregen und zu binden vermag. Sie konnten nur
to arouse and to bind may They could only

überwunden werden durch ein Ideal, wie es in jener
overcome become through an ideal as it in that

herrlichen Zeit aufflammte und mit der Macht einer neuen
great time flared up and with the power of a new

Religion die Geister umfing, einer Religion, welche alle
religion the spirits embraced a religion which all

unhaltbaren und unzeitgemäßen Formen und Dogmen
unsustainable and out of date forms and dogmas

ausschied und jenen unsterblichen Kern des Christentums
retired and that immortal core of the christianity

enthüllte, den ein Kant, ein Schiller vorahnend
revealed that a Kant a Schiller anticipating
(philosopher) (philosopher)

empfunden. Vielleicht hat die Überlegung, dass der
perceived Perhaps has the consideration that the

Einzelne nur im Ganzen zu existieren und zu wirken
individual only in the whole to exist and to act

vermag, dass die heilige Ordnung allein Staaten und
may that the holy order alone states and

48

Menschen erhalten kann, dass nicht das erreichte Ziel,
people contain can that not the reached target

sondern das Streben und Ringen allein das Glück enthält
but the striving and wrestling alone the fortune contains

und dass ein jeder nur sich zufrieden fühlen kann in
and that one each only oneself content feel can in

dem beschränkten Kreise, der die volle Betätigung seiner
the cramped circle which the full activity of his

Energien zulässt und abgrenzt – vielleicht hat diese
energies allows and delimits – perhaps has this

Überlegung jenes Ideal allmählich erzeugt. Aber sie musste
consideration that ideal gradually generated But she had to

erst in einer Reihe von Generationen durch fortschreitende
first in a row from generations through progressive

Vererbung in Fleisch und Blut übergehen, das heißt aus
inheritance in flesh and blood pass over the is called from

einem Schlusse des Verstandes sich verwandeln in ein
a close of the mind itself transform in an

Axiom der sittlichen Anschauung; sie musste zu einem
axiom of the moral view she must to an

Ideale werden, das hoch über allen Wechselfällen der
ideal become that high over all change cases of the
changes

Wirklichkeit als ein unverrückbarer Leitstern jede
reality as an immovable lodestar each

Entschließung   bestimmt,   jeden   Widerspruch
resolution   identified   every   contradiction

verstummen   macht.«
fall silent   make
silenced

»Und   sollte   dies   alles   nicht   auch   durch   einen   Fortschritt
And   should   this   all   not   also   through   a   progress
                      all this

der   Erkenntnis   zu   erreichen   sein?   Durch   die   ausgebildete
of the   understanding   to   reach   be   Through   the   trained

Fähigkeit,   in   einem   Augenblicksschlusse,   ähnlich   den
ability   in   one   instantaneous conclusion   like   the

Schlüssen   des   Taktgefühls,   die   ganze   Reihe   der
conclusion   of the   tact   the   whole   row   of the

Möglichkeiten   zu   überblicken   und   daraus   diejenige
possibilities   to   overlook   and   there from   the one

Bestimmung   zu   treffen,   welche   dem   eigenen   Anspruche   und
determination   to   meet   which   the   own   expectations   and

dem   Recht   der   Allgemeinheit   am   besten   entspricht?   Das
the   right   of the   generality   at the   best   corresponds to   That

aber   ist   ein   intellektueller   Fortschritt,   und   wir   befinden
however   is   a   more intellectual   progress   and   we   find

uns   auf   rein   wissenschaftlichem   Gebiete.   Von   diesem
ourselves   on   clean   scientific   area   From   this

Fortschritt   leite   ich   den   Gesamtfortschritt   der
progress   lead   I   the   overall progress   of the
          (leite ab; deduce)

Menschheit   ab.   Wir   alle   sind   einig   darin,   dass   unser
mankind   off   We   all   are   agreed   therein   that   our

Zeitalter sich auszeichnet durch sein geistiges
age itself distinguishes through its spiritual

Gleichgewicht, durch seinen Edelmut, seine liberale
balance through its gallantry its liberal

Gesinnung, welche es unmöglich macht, in die Niederungen
attitude which it impossible makes in the lowlands

hämischen Streites, zur Absicht beleidigender Kränkung,
(of) malicious arguments to the intention more insulting insult

zurückzukehren. Ich erkläre es geradezu für unmöglich,
to turn back I declare it almost for impossible

dass aus dem Streite entgegengesetzter Meinungen
that from the argument of opposite opinions

heutzutage ein persönlicher Hass, ja nur eine
these days a personal hate yes only an
indeed

tatsächliche Anfeindung hervorgehen könne. Und
actual hostility emerge could And

wodurch haben wir das erreicht?«
where-through have we that attained
because of what

»Durch die Ododik«, warf Aromasia ein.
Through the Ododik threw Aromasia in

»Nein, Liebste, allein durch die Erkenntnis und
No dearest alone through the understanding and

Beherrschung der Natur. Der Mensch, der sich seiner
mastery of the nature The human who himself his

51

Stellung zum Ganzen der Welt bewusst ist, begreift auch
position to the whole of the world conscious is realizes also

zugleich das Verhältnis, in welches er sich gerechter
at the same time the relationship in which he himself (in) just

Weise zu seinen Mitmenschen stellen muss, um auch ihnen
manner to his fellow human place must for also them

die Freiheit der Bewegung zu garantieren. Er begreift,
the freedom of the movement to guarantee He realizes

dass Freiheit nur bestehen kann in vernünftiger Unfreiheit,
that freedom only exist can in more reasonable unfreedom

dass nur die gehorsame Unterwerfung unter das Gesetz
that only the obedient submission under the law

frei zu machen vermag. Diese Einsicht macht uns gerecht,
free to make might This insight makes us fair

tolerant, neidlos, friedliebend, sie erhebt uns so hoch über
tolerant envious peace loving she raises us so high over

jene düsteren Zeiten, in denen schon eine Verschiedenheit
those gloomy times in which already a diversity

der metaphysischen Überzeugung genügte, die wildesten
of the metaphysical convictions satisfied the wildest
(religions and ideologies)

und zerstörendsten Affekte zu entfesseln. Ob man
and most destructive effects to unleash Whether one

dabei Ododion räuchert oder nicht, das ist vollständig
there-by Ododion smokes or not that is totally

gleichgültig.«
indifferent

52

»Oxygen«, sagte Aromasia, »du bist sehr unartig. Ich
Oxygen — said — Aromasia — you — are — very — naughty — I

vermisse wieder einmal den Respekt, den du vor der
miss — again — once — the — respect — that — you — before — the

Kunst haben solltest, welche meine Lebensaufgabe
art — have — should — which — my — life task

ausmacht.«
makes out
exists of

»Beste Aromasia, ich hoffe, du wirst deine Lebensaufgabe
Dear — Aromasia — I — hope — you — will — your — life task

noch anders auffassen lernen.«
still — different — understand — learn

»Niemals, mein Oxygen! Ich kann und darf es nicht
Never — my — Oxygen — I — can — and — may — it — not

dulden, dass du durch deine absprechenden Theorien jedes
tolerate — that — you — through — your — coordinating — theories — each

innige Gefühl mit Füßen trittst. Wenn nicht einmal
intimate — feeling — with — feet — steps (on) — When — not — once

unsere innere Güte und Liebenswürdigkeit, unsere
our — inner — quality — and — kindness — our

Vorurteilslosigkeit und Selbstlosigkeit aus der warmen
unprejudicedness — and — selflessness — from — the — warm

Empfindung unseres Herzens stammen soll, dann musst
sensation — (of) our — heart — come — should — then — must

du auch diese selbst leugnen, und jedes künstlerische
you also this yourself deny and each artistic

Bestreben könnte sich zum Sirius scheren!«
striving could itself to ~~the~~ Sirius shear
chase

»Ich muss Ihnen beistimmen«, sagte Magnet,
I must you agree said Magnet

»Das tut mir Leid«, entgegnete Oxygen, »aber ich erhalte
That does me suffering replied Oxygen but I get

meine Geringschätzung eurer schönen Künste aufrecht. Der
my disregard of your beautiful arts upright The
correct

Schwerpunkt des modernen Lebens kann nur in dem
main emphasis of the modern life can only in the

Fortschritt des Erkennens liegen. Und ich behaupte noch
progress of the recognition lie And I assumed still
knowledge

mehr. Wir werden durch die Wissenschaft dazu kommen,
more We will through the science there-to come

überhaupt jede Kunst aufzuheben und diese Spielereien
at all each art to cancel and these gadgets

überflüssig zu machen.«
superfluous to make

»Oh, oh!«
Oh oh

»Ja, gewiss! Ihr wisst, dass wir durch die Natur unseres
Yes certainly You know that we through the nature (of) our

Erkenntnisvermögens gezwungen sind, alle Veränderungen in
cognitive ability compelled are all changes in

der Erscheinungswelt zurückzuführen auf die Bewegung von
the presence-world / back-to-carry on the movement from
visible world to attribute

Atomen. Licht, Wärme, Elektrizität, chemische
atoms Light warmth electricity chemical

Verwandtschaft, Gravitation und wie immer die einzelnen
relationship gravitation and as always which single

Bewegungsarten des Stoffes heißen, sie alle unterscheiden
types of movement of the fabric are called they all discern

sich nur durch die Größe und Zusammenordnung der
themselves only through the size and order of the

schwingenden Atome und durch die Geschwindigkeit und
swinging atoms and through the speed and

Richtung derselben in ihren Bahnen. Nun kann man die
direction of the same in her courses Now can one the

meisten dieser Schwingungsarten in andere überführen, so
most of these types of vibration in others carry over so

dass jede Eigenschaft der Körper verändert und diese
that each property the body changes and this

ineinander umgewandelt werden. Nehmen wir an, wir
into one another converted become Take we on we
Assume

seien so weit gekommen, dass man jede beliebige
are so far come that one each desired
had

Bewegungsform in jede andere überzuführen vermag –
motion form in each other carry over might –

haben wir nicht dann das Weltall in unserer Hand? Dann
have we not then the space in our hand Then

gilt wirklich das Wort des alten Philosophen nicht
concerns really the word of the old philosopher not
(here Plato)

mehr als ein Widerspruch, dass alles aus allem
(any)more as a contradiction that everything from all

werden kann. Und was sollte dann die vorgeschrittene
become can And what should then the advanced

Menschheit hindern, jene Umgestaltung der
mankind prevent that remodeling of the

Atom-Bewegungen hervorzurufen, durch welche die Atome
atomic movements to evoke through which the atoms

ihre gegenseitigem Bewegungen selbst aufheben? Dann
their mutual movements themselves lift up Then
cancel

wird eine relative Ruhelage derselben entstehen, ein
will a relative rest position of the same arise a

Gleichgewicht der Kräfte – die Körper müssen sich ihrem
balance of the forces – the body must itself her

Wesen nach vernichten und die Welten aus der Existenz
being after destroy and the worlds from the existence

verschwinden, ehe der natürliche Verlauf von selbst zur
disappear before the natural process from itself to the

Erstarrung des Alls führt.«
solidification of the everything leads

»Aber bester Freund, du weist doch, dass die Atome und
But dear friend you know however that the atoms and

ihre Bewegungen eben auch nur unsere Vorstellungen sind,
their movements just also only our imaginations are

dass die ganze Welt in der Form, wie du sie beschreibst,
that the whole world in the form as you she describe

nur als unsere Erscheinung besteht.«
only as our appearance consists

»Eben darum. Sie erscheint uns nun einmal nur in Form
Just therefore she appears us now once only in form

bewegter Atome – was sie an sich ist, bleibt
(of) moved atoms – what she by herself is remains

gleichgültig; heben wir diese Bewegung auf, und
indifferent lift we this movement up and
(aufheben; cancel)

die Erscheinung wird aufgehoben sein. Wir haben es ja
the appearance will lifted up be We have it yes
indeed

nur mit einer phänomenalen Welt zu tun und kennen
only with one phenomenal world to do and know

keine andere; diese aber muss vernichtet werden. Wenn
no other this however must destroyed become When

die Welt für uns nicht mehr existiert, so ist es so gut,
the world for us not (any)more exists so is it so good

als existierte überhaupt nichts.«
as existed at all nothing

»Und was wird aus unserer Empfindung, die doch
And what will from our sensation which indeed

offenbar als die innere Seite des Seins gar nichts mit
obviously as the inner part of the existence at all nothing with

der Bewegung zu tun hat?«
the movement to do has

»Besteht nicht zwischen beiden ein vollständiger
Consists not between both a complete

Parallelismus? Entspricht nicht tatsächlich jedem
parallelism Corresponds to not indeed each

Empfindungsvorgang ein äußerer Bewegungsvorgang, welcher
sensation process an outer movement which

nur das Spiegelbild von jenem inneren ist, erzeugt durch
only the mirror image from that inner one is generated through

unsere äußere Sinnesauffassung in Raum und Stoff?
our outer sense perceiving in space and material

Hebe die Möglichkeit auf, dass das entsteht, was wir
Would lift the possibility on that that arises what we

organisierte Wesen mit Zentralorganen des Bewusstseins
organized beings with central organs of the awareness

nennen, und du hast auch das Bewusstsein in seinen
call and you have also the awareness in its

höheren Formen aufgehoben. Glaubst du, dass der innere
high form lifted up / canceled Believe you that the inner

Bewusstseinsinhalt einer Welt, welche einem äußeren
content of consciousness a world which an outer

Zuschauer, wie uns, nur als eine unzählbare Summe
spectator like us only as an uncountable total

geradlinig nebeneinander durch den Raum ziehender
straightforward side by side through the space pulling

Atome erscheinen würde, dass dieser Bewusstseinsinhalt
atoms appear would that this content of consciousness

noch eine Welt genannt werden kann? In diese Form
still a world called become can in this form

ohne wechselnden Inhalt muss die Welt umsetzbar sein!«
without changing content must the world turnable be

»Und wenn du selbst mit dieser Theorie einer möglichen
And when you yourself with this theory a possible

Selbstvernichtung der Welt Recht hättest, die doch
self-destruction of the world right had which indeed

übrigens nur in einer unabsehbaren Zukunft zu realisieren
by the way only in an unforeseeable future to realize

wäre, wenn wir den leicht zu erhebenden Einwand
would be when we the easy to uplift objection

ganz außer Acht lassen wollten, dass ja doch unser
completely without guard leave wanted that yes indeed our
indeed

menschliches Bewusstsein nicht das Einzige seiner Art in
human awareness not the only of its sort in

der Welt sein dürfte und dass immer und immer Formen
the world be might and that always and always forms

des Seins existieren werden - wie gesagt, abgesehen
of the existence exist will - as said aside

59

von all diesem, so bist du doch immer noch die
from all this so are you indeed always still the

Begründung deiner Geringschätzung unserer Kunst uns
reason of your disregard of our art us

schuldig geblieben. Sind wir es denn nicht, die in diesem
owing remained Are we it then not who in this

unentfliehbaren Mechanismus uns den Rest von Freiheit
inescapable mechanism us the rest of freedom

bewahren, der allein das Leben erträglich macht? Sind
preserve which alone the life bearable makes Are

wir es nicht, die der Menschheit die Rettung aus der
we it not who the mankind the rescue from the

niederdrückenden Schwere der Wirklichkeit in das heitere
depressing heaviness of the reality in the cheerful
weight

Reich des Ideals allein ermöglichen, indem wir alle
kingdom of the ideals alone enable while we all

edleren und zarteren Regungen des Gemütes leiten und
nobler and more delicate emotions of the mind to lead and

beherrschen? Nur durch die Kunst ist es möglich,
to dominate Only through the art is it possible

Stimmung zu erzeugen, das heißt einen Gesamtzustand
mood to produce that is called an overall condition

unseres Seelenlebens hervorzurufen, in welchem wir in
(of) our soul life to evoke in which we in

60

dem Lustgefühl des in sich abgeschlossenen Empfindens
the feeling of pleasure of the in itself closed off feeling senses

gewissermaßen erfahren, was es heißt zu sein.«
(in) certain measure (so to speak) experience what it is called to be

»Diese Rolle eben, welche die Künstler jetzt spielen,
This role just which the artist now plays

werden künftighin die Physiologen übernehmen. Wenn ihr
will in the future the physiologists take over When you

mit euren Kunstwerken die Menschen in eine Stimmung
with your works of art the people in a mood

versetzen wollt, kommt ihr mir vor wie ein Arzt, der
offset want comes you me before as a doctor who

die Aufgabe hat, einen Patienten von einer unverdaulichen
the task has a patient from an indigestible

Speise zu befreien, und ihn zu diesem Zwecke eine
meal to free and him to this purpose a

Seereise unternehmen lässt, damit er die Seekrankheit
sea voyage undertake lets there-with he the seasickness

bekomme. Wie würde dir ein solcher Arzt gefallen? Du
gets How would you a such doctor please You

würdest sagen, warum gibt der Mann nicht lieber ein
would say why gives the man not rather a

direktes Brechmittel? Ihr Künstler seid in derselben Lage,
direct vomit-means You artists are in the same situation
emetic

61

nur kennt ihr eben das einfache, von innen wirkende
only know you just the simple from inside acting

Mittel nicht. Wir werden es auffinden, das heißt, wir
means not We will it find up that is called we
find out is

werden zeigen, wie man das Gehirn unmittelbar in jenen
will demonstrate how one the brain immediately in that

Zustand versetzen kann, den ihr nach großer Mühe
status set can that you after great trouble
bring

vermittels der Sinne durch eure Kunstwerke hervorzurufen
through the sense through your works of art to evoke

versucht. Und darum brauchen wir weder dein Grunzulett
try And therefore need we neither your greentreat

noch deine Riechstückchen.«
nor your smell-pieces
smell-compositions

»Dann muss ich dir freilich überflüssig vorkommen«,
Then must I you indeed superfluous occur to
appear to

erwiderte Aromasia gereizt. »Du redest, als wärest du ein
answered Aromasia irritated You talk as would be you a

Zauberer, der ohne weiteres geschehen lässt, was er will.
wizard that without additional happened lets what he wants

Es soll mich nicht wundern, wenn du nächstens
It should me not wonder when you next (time)

behauptest, man werde noch lernen, sich unsichtbar zu
claim one will still learn oneself invisible to

machen!«
make

»Und das behaupte ich auch.«
And that claim I also

»Ich verstehe dich nicht mehr.«
I understand you not (any)more

Oxygen zuckte die Achseln. Dann sagte er: »Von meiner
Oxygen twitched the shoulders Then said he Of my
shrugged

Überzeugung kann ich nicht abgehen; und so gut ich an
conviction can I not off-go and so good I on
relent as

die dereinstige Selbstvernichtung der Welt und an die
the one day self-destruction of the world and on the

Zukunftslosigkeit der Ododik glaube, ebenso gut glaube
without-future-ness of the Ododik believe likewise good believe
futility

ich, dass die Zukunft die Kunst des Unsichtbarwerdens
I that the future the art of the becoming invisible

erfinden wird.«
to invent will

»So wünschte ich, wir lebten in dieser Zukunft; dann
<small>So wished I we lived in this future then</small>

würde ich mich sofort unsichtbar machen, wenn du so
<small>would I myself immediately invisible make when you so</small>

abscheulich sprichst.«
<small>hideously speaks</small>

»Aromasia, jetzt verstehe ich dich nicht mehr. Ich hoffe,
<small>Aromasia now understand I you not (any)more I hope</small>

du scherzest nur.«
<small>you are kidding only</small>

»Es scheint, dass wir uns nie verstehen werden.
<small>It seems that we ourselves never understand will
each other</small>

Solche Behauptungen kann ich nicht ertragen. Sie
<small>Such claims can I not endure You</small>

widersprechen meinem innersten Wesen.«
<small>disagree (with) my innermost being</small>

»Ich begreife dich auch nicht mehr«, fiel Magnet ein.
<small>I understand you also not (any)more fell Magnet in</small>

»Wie kannst du im Ernste solche Ansichten aussprechen?
<small>How can you in the serious such views pronounce</small>

Jede bürgerliche Existenz müsste dann aufhören, seiner
<small>Each civil existence should then stop his</small>

Person, seines Eigentums wäre niemand sicher. Ich sehe
<small>person of his property would be nobody sure I see</small>

in — eine — Sittenverderbnis — ohnegleichen! — Wenn — ihr
in — a — moral corruption — unparalleled — when — your

›Nüchternen‹ — doch — nicht — in — so — törichter — Weise — glaubtet,
Sober ones — indeed — not — in — such — foolish — manner — believe

das — Geheimnis — des — Seins — von — seinem — Schleier — befreien
the — secret — of the — existence — from — its — veil — to free

zu — können. — Sich — unsichtbar — machen! — Merkt — ihr — denn
to — be able — Oneself — invisible — make — Notice — you — then

nicht, — dass — ihr — dem — Reiche — der — Märchen — und — Hexereien
not — that — you — the — kingdom — of the — fairy tales — and — witchcraft

zusteuert? — Dass — ihr — in — selbstverschuldetem — Kreise — dazu
directs to — That — you — in — self-inflicted — circle — there-to

gelangt, — eure — eigenen — Behauptungen — von — der
reached — your — own — claims — from — the

Gesetzmäßigkeit — der — Natur — aufzuheben? — Ihr — vernichtet — euch
lawfulness / laws — of ~~the~~ — nature — to lift up / to cancel — You — destroy — you

selbst, — ihr — Kurzsichtigen!«
yourself — you — shortsighted one

»Wo — ist — nun — die — Kurzsichtigkeit«, — rief — Oxygen — in — heftigem
Where / So who is — is — now — the — shortsightedness — called — Oxygen — in — violent

Tone, — »bei — euch, — die — ihr — glaubt, — mit — Ododion-Gestänker — die
tone — with — you — that — her — believes — with — Ododion-stinks — the

Welt — glücklich — zu — machen, — oder — bei — uns, — die — wir — bewusst
world — happy — to — make — or — with — us — who — we — deliberately

sie — der — Menschheit — zu — Füßen — legen? — Allerdings — muss — es
her — the — mankind — at — (the) feet — to lay — Of all things / Above all — must — it

65

unser letzter Zweck sein, die Natur aufzuheben, die Atome
our last purpose be ~~the~~ nature to cancel the atoms

in ihre relative Ruhelage zu bringen und zum
in their relative rest position to bring and to the

ursprünglichen Nichts, zum Nullpunkt des Seins,
original nothing to the zero point of the existence

zurückzukehren.«
to return

»Das ist eine Rohheit der Gesinnung«, fuhr Magnet auf,
That is a rawness of the attitude drove Magnet on
way of thinking carried

»mit der du Aromasia, mit der du mich beleidigst! Seit
with which you Aromasia with which you me insult Since

wann ist es Sitte, so rücksichtslos sich zu äußern?«
when is it habit so without disregard oneself to express? «

»Und mit welchem Rechte stellst du mich zur Rede?«,
And with which right put you me to the speech

fragte Oxygen aufstehend.
asked Oxygen getting up

»Ich erteile ihm dies Recht«, rief Aromasia. »Denn gegen
I issue him this right called Aromasia Because against

dich bedarf ich des Schutzes. – Unerhört sind solche
you need I -of the- protection – Outrageous are such

Auftritte   nach   unseren   Schicklichkeitsbegriffen.   Ich   gehe.
occurrences   to   our   understanding of decency   I   go
behaviors

Begleiten   Sie   mich,   Magnet.«
Escort   you   me   Magnet

Die   Gesellschaft   trennte   sich.
The   company   separated   itself

Aromasia   und   Magnet   warfen   sich   in   eine   Luftdroschke
Aromasia   and   Magnet   threw   themselves   in   an   airboat

und   flogen   nach   Aromasias   Wohnung.
and   flew   to   Aromasia's   house

»Es   ist   schändlich!«,   sagte   Magnet.   »Oxygen,   der
It   is   shameful   said   Magnet   Oxygen   the

›Nüchterne‹,   der   große   Mann   des   vierundzwanzigsten
Sober ones   the   great   man   of the   twenty-fourth

Jahrhunderts,   der   eben   das   Wort   gesprochen: Ich   erkläre
century   who   just   the   word   spoken (has)   I   declare

einen   persönlichen   Streit   aus   theoretischer
a   personal   conflict   out (of)   theoretical

Meinungsverschiedenheit   für   unmöglich!   Wo   ist   hier   jene
disagreement   for   impossible   Where   is   here   that

selige   Ruhe   des   Gemüt,   die   aus   der   Erkenntnis   fliegen
blessed   rest   of the   mind   that   from   the   understanding   fly
calml   flow out

soll?   Gehässige   Angriffe   gegen   das,   was   das   Heiligste   für
should   Spiteful   attacks   against   that   what   the   most sacred   for

unsere Empfindung ist, Verletzung unserer innersten
our sensation is Injury of our innermost

Interessen, das nennt er Objektivität der Betrachtung!
interests that calls he objectivity of the consideration

Weinen Sie nicht, Aromasia! Er ist der Absonderung Ihrer
Cry you not Aromasia He is the secretion of your

Tränendrüsen nicht wert, welche die Kapillaranziehung
tear glands not worth which the capillary attraction

Ihrer Augenwimpern nur mühsam gegenüber der
of your eye lashes only tediously against the

Schwerkraft der Erde zurückhält! Weinen Sie nicht –
gravity of the earth hold back Cry you not –

setzen Sie sich ans Ododion, hier spielen Sie!«
set you yourself to the Ododion here play you

Aromasia sprang auf.
Aromasia jumped on

»Nein«, rief sie mit blitzenden Augen, »er ist der Trauer
No called she with flashing eyes he is the mourning

nicht wert! Oh, ich wusste es – ein Nüchterner! Ich
not worth Oh I knew it – a Sober one I

wusste es! Aber – Rache!«
knew it But – Revenge

»Bleiben Sie ruhig, Aromasia, ich werde Sie rächen! Sie
stay you calm Aromasia I will you revenge You

und mich! Ich werde uns rächen, wie es die Gesetze der
and myself I will us revenge as it the laws of the

Ehre erfordern, aber schärfer, als er es erwarten wird.
honor require but sharper as he it expect will

Räuchern Sie, fantasieren Sie – ich sammle dabei meine
Smoke you fantasize you – I gather there-by my

Gedanken. Oxygen weiß sehr wohl, dass wir an die
thoughts Oxygen knows very well that we to the

öffentliche Meinung appellieren müssen und werden; aber
public opinion appeal must and will but

wie, wie wir ihn zerschmettern – das kann er nicht
how how we him crush – that can he not

ahnen. Schon dämmert mir's! Aromasia – Sie spielen
suspect Already dawns me it Aromasia – You play

bezaubernd!«
adorable

Aromasia saß am Ododion und fantasierte. Groll, Hass,
Aromasia sat at the Ododion and fantasized resentment hate

Verzweiflung sprachen aus den betäubenden,
despair spoke from the numbing

nasezermalmenden Düften und rissen den Zuriechenden
nose crushing smell and tore the smelling one

unwiderstehlich hin, bis sich alles im tiefen Schmerz
irresistibly away until itself everything in the deep pain

der enttäuschten Liebe auflöste.
of the disappointed love dissolved

Magnet aber ruhte im Hängestuhl und sann auf
Magnet however rested in the hammock chair and contemplated on

das anklagende Rachegedicht gegen Oxygen. Auf dem
the accusatory revenge poem against Oxygen On the

Nullpunkt des Seins wollte er ihn darstellen, wie er
zero point of the existence wanted he him represent how he

ganz allein existierend ohne Raum und Zeit unsichtbar
completely alone existing without space and time invisible

auf den gleichfalls unsichtbaren Leichnamen der Kunst
on the also invisible corpses of the art

und Sitte Hullu-Kullu tanzte! Das war der neueste
and morals Hullu-Kullu danced That was the newest

Modetanz, dessen Pointe im Zusammenrennen der
fashion dance of which the point in the running together of the

Köpfe bestand.
heads existed

Eilig schrieb er über den Zeilen des Gedichts. Schon
Hurriedly wrote he over the lines of the poem Already

in der nächsten Stunde sollte es auf allen öffentlichen
in the next hour should it on all public

Zeitungstafeln an den Ecken durch telegrafischen
newspaper boards on the corners through telegraphic

Selbstdruck erscheinen. Es musste eine niederschmetternde
self press appear It must a devastating
print on demand

Wirkung üben und den Angegriffenen in Gesellschaft und
effect practice and the attacked one in company and
have

70

Welt vernichten. Heute Abend, wenn Aromasia im
world destroy Today evening when Aromasia in the

Odoratorium spielte, musste sich die Wirkung zeigen.
odoratorium played must itself the effect demonstrate

Triumphierend las Magnet sein Produkt Aromasia vor,
Triumphantly read Magnet his product Aromasia before
to

welche es ododramatisch begleitete.
which it ododramatically accompanied
with dramatic smells

Widerstrebende Empfindungen kämpften in Aromasias
Conflicting sensations struggled in Aromasia's
emotions

Herzen; zu ihren Füßen saß Magnet, zufrieden und
heart at her feet sat Magnet, content and

glücklich im Gefühl der befriedigten Rache und der
happy in the feeling of the satisfied revenge and the

innigsten Anbetung der Künstlerin, welche aus Essigäther
most intimate worship of the artist which from vinegar

und Zwiblozin die herrlichsten Gase mischte und den
and zwiblozin the most delicious gases mixed and the

Augen heiße Tränen entlockte. Draußen aber, an den
eyes hot tears elicited Outside however on the
through

Türritzen, an den Fensterspalten, an den Öffnungen
door slits on the window frames on the openings
through through

71

des   Rauchfangs,   drängte   sich   die   duftsaugende   Menge,
of the   smoke trap   penetrated   itself   the   fragrant   masses
     chimney

die   bezaubernden   Fantasien   der   großen   Ododistin   zu
the   bewitching   fantasies   of the   large   Ododist   to

erhaschen.
catch

Die Rache im Odoratorium
The Revenge In the Odoratorium

Das Odoratorium, die Stätte für öffentliche
The Odoratorium the site for public

Geruchs-Aufführungen, war zu Konzertsaal und Theater als
smell-performances was to/as concert hall and theater as

ein unentbehrlicher Erholungsort getreten. Es war das
an indispensable place of recreation stepped/become It was the

berühmteste und besuchteste Odoratorium der Stadt, für
most famous and most visited Odoratorium of the city for

welches Aromasia dauernd engagiert war. An einem Tage
which Aromasia constantly engaged was On a day

wie dem heutigen, an welchem man Aromasias Auftreten
as the today (one) on which one Aromasia's performance

angekündigt hatte, wurde die Kasse schon am Morgen
announced had became the cash register already at the morning

von dichten Mengen Riechbegieriger belagert, zumal es
from a close amount of smell eager (people) besieged since it

in der Natur der Ododik lag, dass die Odoratorien nur
in the nature of the Ododism lay that the Odoratoriums only

für eine verhältnismäßig geringe Zahl von Zuriechern
for a relatively small number of smell-tators / smellers

gebaut werden konnten. So hatte die Aufsichtsbehörde
built become could So had the supervisory authority

73

genug zu tun, um die allzu kunsteifrigen Luftvelozipedisten
enough to do for the all too art-eager air-bicyclists

zurückzuhalten, welche durchaus über die Köpfe der
to hold back which throughout over the heads of the
                        at all

Harrenden hinweg in das Ausgabefenster dringen wollten.
waiting away in the outgive-window penetrate wanted
                        ticket window

Eine Stunde vor Beginn des odoratorischen Konzerts –
One hour before beginning of the odoratory concerts –

wie diese Verbindungen von Ododionspiel und Musik
as these connections of Ododion play and music
        combinations

hießen – waren Eintrittskarten bereits nicht mehr zu
were called – were entry-cards already not (any)more to
                tickets

erhalten. Aber heute trat zu dem zu erwartenden
become But today stepped to the to expected
                was added

Kunstgenuss auch noch ein anderes Motiv, welches das
enjoyment of art also still an other motive which the

Publikum auf den Abend begierig machte, nämlich die
audience on the evening eager made namely the

Aussicht auf irgendein Besonderes, Ungewöhnliches, einen
view on any special unusual (thing) a
expectation

Streit, einen kleinen Skandal – man vermutete
conflict a small scandal – one guessed

Verschiedenes. Denn wie geschäftig und ruhelos die Zeit
various (things) / Then, Since / as / busy / and / restless / the / time

auch war, immer hatte sie doch Muße genug, den
also / was / always / had / she / indeed / idleness / enough / the

Privatangelegenheiten der Persönlichkeit von öffentlicher
private matters / of the / personality / from / public

Wirksamkeit ihre Aufmerksamkeit zu schenken, und viele
effectiveness / her / attention / to / give / and / many

fanden ein Vergnügen daran, dem Spiele hinter den
found, experienced / a / pleasure / to it, in it / the / play / behind / the

Kulissen mindestens beizuwohnen, wenn sie nicht selbst
backdrops / at least / to attend / when / she / not / themselves

daran mitwirken konnten.
to it / participate / could

Ein wundersames Gemisch von doktrinärem Ernst und
A / miraculous / mixture / of / doctrinal / seriousness / and

naiver Rücksichtslosigkeit steckte in diesem Zeitalter, wie
more naive / ruthlessness / stuck / in / this / age / as

es uns nicht recht begreiflich erscheint. Aber die letztere
it / us / not / right / understandable / appears / But / the / latter

erklärt sich daraus, dass die Potenzierung der Kultur in
explains / itself / there from / that / the / potentiation / the / culture / in

einer gewissen Beziehung die Gesellschaft der natürlichen
a / certain / relationship / the / company / the / natural

Unabhängigkeit der Individuen wieder genähert hatte. Und
independence / the / individual / again / approached / had / and

75

so müssen wir dieser Geschichte manche Wunderlichkeit nachsehen.

Es war nichts Ungewöhnliches, dass man zwischen den geschäftlichen Nachrichten und den Anzeigen der Vergnügungen auf den öffentlichen Tafeln Angriffe und Rechtfertigungen von Privatpersonen gemischt fand. Hatte doch schon das Neumittelalter, ob es gleich auf die Macht der Dampfpresse in den Zeitungen allein angewiesen war, diesen Weg eingeschlagen, die öffentliche Meinung zum Schiedsrichter in Privatstreitigkeiten zu machen, ja selbst für lange gereimte Nachrufe Teilnahme von ihr verlangt. Freilich galt diese Art der Öffentlichkeit damals nicht gerade für ein Zeichen von

feinerem Takt oder geläutertem Geschmack. Aber man
fine tact or refined taste But one

würde auch sehr irren, wenn man bei der »öffentlichen
would also very be wrong when one at the public

Meinung« der Zeit Aromasias an jenes vielköpfige
opinion in the time of Aromasia on / of that many-headed

Ungeheuer von damals denken wollte, in welchem gerade
monster from that time think wanted in which just

die borniertesten Häupter am lautesten schrien und
the most narrow-minded chief at the loudest screamed and

vor dem Lärm der unverständigen Menge die Stimme
before / because of the noise of the unwise / senseless mass the voice

des Einsichtigen nicht zur Geltung kam. Da die
of those with insight not to the validity / heard was came There the

Hilfsmittel der geistigen Mitteilung durch die Elektrotypie
tools of the intellectual sharing / telling through the electrotype

jegliches Erkennen so sehr erleichterten und der
any recognition so very relieved and the

Bildungsgrad der Masse ein höherer geworden war, so
level of education of the mass(es) / people a higher (one) become was so

konnte auch das Urteil des Einzelnen als ein
could also the judgement of the individual as a

gereifteres, seine Einsicht in den Zusammenhang der
more mature his insight in the context the

Ereignisse als eine tiefere gelten. Jegliche Nachricht ward
events as a deeper be valid / be seen Any message became

im Nu verbreitet, jegliche Erfahrung zum Allgemeingut
in the now / present spread any experience to the common good

gemacht. Zu diesen äußerlichen Hilfsmitteln aber trat
made To these outward tools however stepped / added

ein inneres, im Geiste dieser bevorzugten Zeit liegendes
an inner (one) in the spirit of this favored / advanced time lying

Moment. Es war ein Ideal, das die Menschheit
moment It / There was an ideal that ~~the~~ mankind

beherrschte und für welches es gegenwärtig keinen rechten
mastered and for which it currently no right

Namen gibt. Ein mächtiges, tief eingewurzeltes
name gives An powerful / enormous deep rooted

Pflichtgefühl, ein allgemein verbreiteter, eigentümlicher
feeling of duty a generally more common peculiar

Ehrbegriff wirkten zusammen, um das Bewusstsein von
concept of honor worked together for the awareness from

dem Werte der Menschheit und der gegenseitigem
the values of ~~the~~ mankind and the mutual

Unentbehrlichkeit ihrer Glieder aus einer schönen Phrase
indispensability of its members from a beautiful phrase

78

zu einer unabweichlichen Richtschnur des Handelns zu
to an inevitable guideline of the act to

machen.
make

So konnte auch die Meinung der Gesamtheit geklärt und
So could also the opinion of the entirety clarified and

dem Irrtum minder unterworfen sein, so konnte es
to the mistake less subjected be so could it

geschehen, dass sie in der Tat zu einer Macht
happen that she in the deed to a power
indeed

emporgestiegen war, der niemand sich zu entziehen
climbed up was that nobody itself to pull away

vermochte. Die Zahl der Verbrechen und Vergehen hatte
could The number of the crimes and offenses had

ungemein abgenommen; gab es doch kaum noch Mittel,
ungeneric decreased gave it indeed hardly still means
immensely were there

sie zu verheimlichen. Würde es immer so bleiben? Gewiss
them to conceal Would it always so remain Certainly

nicht. Gegenwärtig aber war die menschliche Gesellschaft
not Currently however was ~~the~~ human society

auf einem glücklichen Höhepunkte ihrer Entwicklung
on a happy high-point of her development

angelangt. Wenn noch mitunter Verstöße gegen die
arrived When still with-under violations against the
every now and then

Gesetze vorkamen, so genügte es meistens, dass die
laws occurred so satisfied it mostly that the

öffentliche Meinung den Schuldigen verurteilte, und er war
public opinion the guilty-ones condemned and he was

sicherer unschädlich gemacht, ja vielleicht strenger
sure harmless made yes perhaps more severe

bestraft, als wenn ihn das Gefängnis eingeschlossen hätte.
punished as when him the jail locked in had

Die öffentliche Meinung war nicht mehr ein blindes
The public opinion was not (any)more a blind

Urteil der Menge, sie war der konzentrierte Ausdruck
judgement of the mass(es) she was the concentrated expression
people

einer Überzeugung der Menschen nach bester und
of a conviction of the people to most best and

aufrichtigster Einsicht.
most sincere insight

Wie tief beleidigt musste Aromasia sein, dass sie Magnet
How deeply offended must Aromasia be that she Magnet

gestattete, Oxygen der öffentlichen Meinung preiszugeben!
allowed Oxygen the public opinion price-to-give
to expose

Ja, ihr Name stand ebenfalls unter dem Gedichte des
Yes her name stood likewise under the poems of the

Angreifers. Anonymität kannte man nicht, sie wurde
attacker anonymity knew one not she became
(anonymity)

auch von der öffentlichen Meinung nicht anerkannt; und
also from the public opinion not accepted and

jene uns geläufige Scheu vor der Öffentlichkeit gab es
that to us familiar shyness before the openness gave it
of publicity

im vierundzwanzigsten Jahrhundert überhaupt nicht.
in the twenty-fourth century at all not

Die Appellationen an die öffentliche Meinung, welche, wie
The appellations to the public opinion which as

gesagt, etwas Alltägliches waren, machten im
said something everyday were made in the

Allgemeinen kein Aufsehen; denn es waren immer nur
general not (a) sensation then it were always only
since

kleinere und zunächst interessierte Kreise, welche über
smaller and to-closest interested circles which over
mostly

gewöhnliche Angriffe und Anklagen ihr Urteil sprachen
ordinary attacks and accusations their judgement spoke

und durch ihr moralisches Gewicht entschieden. Heute
and through their moral weight decided. Today

aber hatten die Chiffren des Elektrotyps, als sie auf
however had the ciphers of the electrotype as they on

den großen Tafeln sich abdruckten, eine
the large signboards themselves printed an

außerordentliche Bewegung hervorgerufen. Denn erstens
extraordinary movement evoked Then first (of all)

war der Angriff selbst ebenso gewandt und trefflich
was the attack itself likewise agile and excellent

81

abgefasst als beißend und vernichtend; zweitens war er
drafted as biting and devastating second was he
it

von dem bekannten Dichter Magnet Reimert-Oberton und
from the famous poet Magnet Rhymer-Overtone and

der beliebten Ododistin Aromasia Duftemann-Ozodes
the popular Ododist Aromasia Duftemann-Ozode

unterzeichnet; drittens war er gegen einen verdienten und
undersigned thirdly was he against a deserved and
it

weit über die Grenzen seines Wohnortes hinaus
far over the borders of his place of residence out

allgemein geachteten Bürger, den Wetterfabrikanten Oxygen
generally respected civilian the weather manufacturer Oxygen

Warm-Blasius gerichtet, und viertens war dieser, wie
Warm-Blasius directed and fourthly was this one as

jedermann wusste, der verlobte Bräutigam der Künstlerin.
everyone knew the engaged bridegroom of the artist

Dazu kam noch, dass man aus der äußeren Form
There-to came still that one from the outer form

erkannte, wie ernsthaft der Angriff gemeint sei. Denn
recognized how serious the attack meant be Then

während sonst die längste Zeitdauer, während welcher
while otherwise the longest duration during which

man eine solche Ankündigung an den öffentlichen Tafeln
one a such announcement on the public signboards
they

stehen ließ, fünfzig Minuten betrug, waren bereits zwei
stand let fifty minutes carried were already two
took

Stunden verflossen, seitdem Aromasias und Magnets Gedicht
hours passed since then Aromasia's and Magnets poem

an den Ecken glänzte. Da lag ein Ereignis zu Grunde,
on the corners shone There lay an event to ground

über dessen Motive man nicht so rasch wie gewöhnlich
over which motive one not so quickly as usually

klar wurde, und undeutliche Gerüchte aus dem
clear became and indistinct rumors from the

Pyramidenhotel vermehrten noch die Unsicherheit. Erst
pyramid hotel increased still the insecurity First

musste Oxygen replizieren, ehe man über die Sachlage
must Oxygen reply before one over the situation

urteilen durfte.
to judge was allowed

Mit Spannung erwartete man, was Oxygen auf diesen
With tension expected one what Oxygen on this

Angriff beginnen werde. Einige meinten, dass sich nach
attack begin will Some thought that itself after

einer Aufklärung des Sachverhaltes und einer öffentlichen
a reconnaissance of the facts and a public

Rechtfertigung die allgemeine Ansicht zu Oxygens Gunsten
justification the general opinion to Oxygen's favor

neigen würde; auch eine so beliebte Persönlichkeit wie
tend would also a so popular personality as

Aromasia dürfe nicht geschont werden, wenn der Angriff
Aromasia might not spared become when the attack

sich als ungerecht herausstellen sollte.
itself as unfair point out should

Andere jedoch, welche Oxygens Stolz, seine Hartnäckigkeit
Others however which Oxygen's pride his tenacity

und leichte Reizbarkeit kannten, vermuteten, dass dieser
and light irritability knew suspected that this

ungewöhnliche Mann, welcher der Natur so viel
unusual man which the nature so much

abzutrotzen wusste, hier der gesellschaftlichen Gewohnheit
to wrestle from knew here the social habits

sich nicht fügen, sondern eine Rache auf eigene Faust
itself not suit but a revenge on own fist

versuchen würde.
try would

Als Oxygen den gegen ihn gerichteten Angriff las, wurde
As Oxygen the against him directed attack read became

er tief bestürzt. Dass ein rein theoretischer Streit, wie
he deeply dismayed That a clean theoretical conflict as

der stattgehabte nach seiner Ansicht war, eine so tiefe
the having place one to his opinion was a so deep

Gemütsbewegung hervorrufen könne, hatte er nicht
mood movement cause could had he not

geglaubt. Bis jetzt hatte er dem Zwischenfall überhaupt
believed Until now had he the incident at all

84

keine größere Bedeutung beigemessen. Aromasias Zürnen
no bigger meaning attached Aromasia anger

hielt er für eine plötzliche Aufwallung, die ebenso leicht
held he for a sudden upsurge that likewise easy

vorübergehen würde, wie sie entstanden war. Heute Abend
pass would as she arose was Today evening

wollte er ihr versöhnend entgegentreten, und sie würde
wanted he her reconciling meet and she would

die angebotene Hand gewiss nicht ausschlagen.
the offered hand certainly not knock out
knock away

Aber nun war es anders gekommen! Auf diese Beleidigung,
But now was it different come On this insult
happened

die ihm jetzt zugefügt war, konnte er nicht den ersten
which him now added was could he not the first
given

Schritt tun. Oder doch? War nicht Aromasia nur
step do Or indeed Was not Aromasia only

irregeführt, hatte er sie nicht gereizt? Und dieser Magnet?
misled had he her not irritated And this Magnet

Sollte er ein Schurke, ein Verräter sein? Hatte er in
Should he a villain a traitor be Had he in

Aromasia den Funken des Hasses geschürt und in
Aromasia the spark of the hate stoked and in

frevelhafter Selbstsucht sie zum Bruche der Treue
more wicked selfishness her to the break of the troth

verleitet? Sicherlich – ihm mußte Rache und Strafe
tempted surely – him must revenge and (a) punishment

gelten!
be valid
be for

Ja, Aromasia war gewiss unschuldig. Nur in einer
Yes Aromasia was certainly innocent Only in an

unstatthaften Erregung des Augenblicks konnte sie das
improper excitement of the moment could she the

verhängnisvolle Pamphlet unterschrieben haben. Und worin
fatal pamphlet signed have And where in

lag der Grund, der dieses reich begabte Weib zu solcher
lay the reason the this richly gifted woman to such
talented

Verblendung hinreißen konnte? Oxygen war keinen
(a) delusion sweep away could Oxygen was no

Augenblick im Zweifel, dass er die Ursache einzig der
moment in the doubt that he the root cause only the

unüberwindlichen Neigung seiner Braut zur Ododik
insurmountable tilt of his bride to the Ododik

zuschreiben müsse. Die unglückselige Geruchskunst war es,
ascribe must The unfortunate Smell-art was it

welche sie von ihm trennte, welche immer wieder aufs
which her from him separated which always again on the

Neue den Streit ihrer entgegengesetzten Anschauungen
new the conflict of her opposite-set views

heraufbeschwören musste. Konnte er denn dieser
conjure up had to Could he then this

86

Leidenschaft Aromasias nicht entgegenarbeiten? Gab es
passion of Aromasia not counteract Gave it
Were there

kein Mittel, das ihr die Ododik gründlich verleiden könnte?
no means that her the Ododik thoroughly suffer could
remove

Wenn es gelänge! Wenn Aromasia die Möglichkeit
When it would succeed When Aromasia the possibility

genommen würde, ihre Kunst auszuüben und damit
taken would her art to exercise and there-with

vielleicht zugleich ihre Liebe zu derselben verloren
perhaps at the same time her love to the same lost

ginge? Sie würde gewiss im Anfang sehr unglücklich
went She would certainly in the beginning very unhappy

sein, aber sie würde sich trösten. Seine Liebe sollte ihr
be but she would herself comfort His love should her

das geraubte Geruchsklavier ersetzen, und in dauernder
the stolen Smell-piano replace and in more permanent

Freude würde sie den einmaligen Schmerz vergessen. Und
joy would she the one-time pain forget And

eine Strafe hatte sie verdient.
a (a) punishment had she earned

Doch vor allem galt es, Magnet
Indeed before all meant it Magnet

zur Rechenschaft zu ziehen!
to the accountability to pull
to make accountable

Aber wie sollte Oxygen dies alles anfangen! Zunächst war
But as should Oxygen this all start First was
do

er der Angeklagte, er hatte sich vor der öffentlichen
he the accused he had himself before the public

Meinung zu verteidigen. Oxygens Empfinden war zu eng
opinion to defend Oxygen's feeling was too close

mit dem seiner Zeit verwachsen, als dass er nicht
with that of his time grown into as that he not

zunächst an dies höchste Gericht hätte denken müssen. Es
first on this highest court had think must It

wurde ihm nicht leicht, von den Gedanken sich zu
became him not light, from the thoughts himself to
was easy

trennen, dass eine Auflehnung gegen diese Verkörperung
separate that a rebellion against this personification

des Zeitgeistes ein Vergehen sei, dass eine Abweichung
of the spirit of time a pass away be that a deviation

von der allgemeinen Sitte seine eigene Verurteilung
from the general habit of his own conviction

herbeiführen müsse. Und doch musste er sich sagen,
bring about must And indeed must he himself say

dass der Ausspruch der öffentlichen Meinung, so
that the out-speak of the public opinion so
judgement

vernichtend er für den Betroffenen war, in diesem
devastating he for the affected was in this

besonderen Fall ihm nicht genügen konnte.
special case him not enough be could

Was hatte die öffentliche Meinung an Aromasia oder
What had the public opinion on/against Aromasia or

gar an Magnet zu verdammen? Doch nur ihren
at all on/against Magnet to condemn Indeed only their

ungerechten Angriff und die persönliche Beleidigung gegen
unjust attack and the personal insult against

Oxygen. Aber der Begriff einer solchen rein
Oxygen But the understanding of a such purely

äußerlichen Verletzung des Selbstgefühls wurde nicht zu
outward Injury of the self-confidence became not too

hoch angeschlagen. Aromasia wäre vielleicht genötigt
high struck/judged Aromasia would be perhaps compelled

worden, auf einige Wochen sich zurückzuziehen, die Stadt
become on/for some weeks herself withdraw the city

zu meiden – wenn sie zurückkehrte, so konnte sie gewiss
to avoid – when she returned so could she certain

sein, dass der Auftritt vergessen und gesühnt sei, dass
be that the performance/deed forgotten and atoned for be/were that

89

sie mit dem früheren Jubel wieder aufgenommen und in
she with the earlier rejoicing again taken up and in
old

alter Weise verehrt werde. Und Magnet – er hatte noch
old manner adored would be And Magnet – he had still

den Milderungsgrund, dass er der beleidigten Aromasia
the mitigation reason that he the insulted Aromasia

sich nur angenommen, dass er nur um ihretwillen in den
himself only on-took that he only for for her sake in the
honored

Streit sich gemischt habe.
conflict himself mingled have

Aber dass Oxygen Aromasia liebte, dass er in dieser Liebe
But that Oxygen Aromasia loved that he in this love

gekränkt und seine schönste Hoffnung ihm vernichtet
hurt and his most beautiful hope of him destroyed

war, die Hoffnung und das Vertrauen auf die milde,
was the hope and the trust on the mild

verzeihende Gemütsart seiner Braut, dass Magnet sicherlich
forgiving temperament of his bride that Magnet surely

die Schuld trug an diesem Wechsel ihrer Gesinnung, dass
that debt carried for this change of her attitude that

dieser Mensch Aussicht hatte, ihm von der Geliebten
this human view had him from the beloved
the plan

vorgezogen zu werden – das waren Anklagegründe, welche
preferred to become – that were charges which

die öffentliche Meinung bei ihrem Urteil nicht in
the public opinion at her judgement not in

Betracht ziehen konnte, nicht einmal sollte.
consideration pull could not once should
even

Dazu aber kam, was sich Oxygen selbst nicht recht
There-to however came what himself Oxygen himself not right

eingestehen wollte, als ein wichtiges Motiv seines
admit wanted as an important motive of his

Rachegefühls die Verstimmung über die Enttäuschung,
revenge the upset over the disappointment

welche seine heiligste, wissenschaftliche Überzeugung
which his most sacred scientific conviction

erlitten hatte. Auf die Leidenschaftslosigkeit der Menschen
suffered had On the dispassion of the people

hatte er gebaut, und hier hatte er sein Spiel völlig
had he built and here had he his play totally

verloren. Das erregte seinen Ingrimm. »Nein«, dachte er,
lost That excited his wrath No thought he

»jenes Gericht der öffentlichen Meinung ist gut und
that court of the public opinion is good and

weise – unter den vorliegenden Verhältnissen jedoch
wise – under the present conditions however

vermag es mich nicht zu befriedigen. Es gibt kein
is able it me not to satisfy It gives no
There is

Gesetz, das in meinem Falle maßgebend und versöhnend
law that in my case authoritative and reconciling

sein könnte. Wie glücklich wart ihr doch, Männer
be could How happy were you indeed men

vergangener Jahrhunderte! Wenn euch eine Beleidigung
of the past centuries When you an insult

zustieß, welche durch das Prozessverfahren der Gerichte
struck which through the litigation of the courts
happened

für euer Gefühl nicht gesühnt werden konnte, so stand
for Your feeling not atoned for become could so stood

euch ein ausreichender Weg immer noch offen. Mit eurem
you a more sufficient way always still open With your

eigenen Leben fordertet ihr das des Gegners heraus.
own life demand you that of the opponent out

Wenn die Gerechtigkeit für euch die Waage nicht ins
When the justice for you the weights not in the

Gleichgewicht zu bringen vermochte, so bot euch der
balance to bring could so offered you the

Zweikampf das letzte Mittel, eure eigene Persönlichkeit in
duel the last means your own personality in

die Schale zu werfen, und ihr waret gerächt oder
the bowl to throw and you were avenged or
weighing

vernichtet. Ich wünschte, ich wäre an eurer Stelle!
destroyed I wished I would be on your spot

Heute? Wenn ich an jenen Gebrauch dächte, ich wurde
Today When I on that use thought I became

ein Gegenstand des Gelächters oder der Verachtung, wenn
an object of the laughter or the despise when

man nicht vorzöge, mich nach Sokotra, der großen
one not preferred me to Sokotra the large

Irren-Insel, zu bringen.
mad people island to bring

Was also bleibt mir übrig als die Rache, welche ich mir
What thus remains to me over as the revenge which I my

selbst nehme. Gut, du hast den Zweikampf mit den
self take Good you have the duel with the

Waffen des Geistes begonnen, ich werde mit den Waffen
weapons of the mind begun I will with the weapons

des Geistes ihn fortsetzen! Aber erlaube, dass ich
of the mind him continue But allow that I
it

diejenigen wähle, welche mir so geläufig sind wie dir
those choose which me so familiar are as (for) you

die deinen, Reimert-Oberton. Du hast deine Reimkunst ins
the yours Rhymer-Overtone YOu have your rhyming art in the

Gefecht geführt - heraus denn, meine zaubermächtige
battle carried - out then my magical

Dienerin, Chemie!
maid chemistry

Es wird gelingen! Ich kenne seinen Platz genau - er ist
It will succeed I know his place exactly - he is

dicht hinter der Rückwand des großen Ododion -, hier
close behind the back wall of the large Ododion -, here

muss der volle Strom ihn treffen«, er murmelte eine
must the full flow him hit he murmured a

chemische Formel, »das genügt! Und Aromasia wird die
chemical formula That is sufficient And Aromasia will the

Lust verlieren, ihre Geruchskünste weiter fortzusetzen. So
desire lose her olfactory arts further to continue So

muss es gehen! Das Publikum freilich – aber was
must it go The audience indeed – but what

kümmert mich das?«
matters me that

Oxygen eilte in das Privat-Laboratorium seiner Fabrik.
Oxygen hurried in the private laboratory of his factory

»Sind die Ododion-Einsätze für Fräulein Duftemann schon
Are the Ododion deployments for miss Fragrantman already

abgeholt?«, fragte er.
picked up asked he

»Nein«, war die Antwort.
No was the answer

»Es ist gut«, sagte er. »Fräulein Duftemann wünscht
It is good said he The young lady Duftemann wishes
That (Fragrantman)

eine schärfere Stimmung. – Sie können gehen, Äthyl, ich
a sharper mood – she can go Aethyl I

brauche keine Hilfe, ich werde die Änderung selbst
need no help I will the modification myself

vornehmen.«
make. «

Oxygen war allein und arbeitete mit Eifer an dem Inhalt
Oxygen was alone and worked with zeal on the content

der Füllbüchsen. Von Zeit zu Zeit trat er in ein sonst
the filling cans from time to time stepped he in an otherwise

von ihm sorgfältig verschlossen gehaltenes Nebenkabinett,
from him carefully locked kept adjoining cabinet
by

wo außer einigen kostbaren und gefährlichen Präparaten
where except for some precious and dangerous preparations

ein eigentümlicher, geheimnisvoller Apparat sich befand.
a peculiar more mysterious machine itself found

Auch mit diesem machte er sich zu schaffen.
also with this one made he himself to create
work

»Für alle Fälle!«, murmelte er bei sich.
For all cases murmured he by himself
Just in case

Eine durchsichtige Hohlkugel in der Hand begab er sich
a transparent hollow sphere in the hand went he himself

an eines der nach Osten gerichteten Fenster. Vorsichtig
on one of the to (the) east directed window Carefully

legte er sie auf die äußere Brüstung und leitete einen
put he her on the outer parapet and led a

Gasstrom aus einem bereitgehaltenen Gasometer darauf.
gas flow from one kept ready gasometer thereupon

Fünf Sekunden vergingen, die Kugel geriet in ein
Five seconds passed the bullet became in a
started

95

schwaches, phosphoreszierendes Leuchten – dann flog sie
weak phosphorescent shining – then flew she

plötzlich mit großer Geschwindigkeit geradlinig nach
suddenly with great speed straightforward to

Osten, sie verschwand im Nu vom Fenster, ohne
(the) east she disappeared in the now from the window without

dass man irgend wahrgenommen hätte, wie die Bewegung
that one anything noticed had how the movement

ihr mitgeteilt worden sei.
her communicated become be

Oxygen nickte zufrieden. »Die alte Erde dreht sich noch«,
Oxygen nodded satisfied The old earth turns itself still

sagte er lächelnd. Dann wandte er sich wieder zu den
said he smiling Then turned he himself again to the

Füllflaschen.
filling bottles

Die Nachbarschaft der Fabrik beklagte sich heute über
The neighborhood of the factory complained itself today over

die abscheulichen Gerüche, welche den Aufenthalt in der
the hideous smells which the stay in the

Nähe unerträglich machten.
proximity unbearable made

Es war Abend geworden, die Laternen an all den leichten
It was evening become the lanterns on all the light
had

Räderwerken, welche die Luft durchschwirrten, waren
wheel works which the air swarmed through were

entzündet, und wie ein Meer von Funken wogte und
ignited and as a lake of sparks surged and

flimmerte es über der Stadt. Abendliche Spazierfahrer
flickered it over the city Evening strollers

stiegen bis zur Grenze des Erdschattens empor, das
climbed until to the limit of the earth shadow up the

Schauspiel der Abendröte noch einmal zu genießen oder
spectacle of the sunset still once to enjoy or

der Sonne noch länger ins glühende Antlitz zu schauen.
the sun still longer in the glowing face to watch

In der Stadt aber flammte es plötzlich auf wie
In the city however blazed it suddenly up as

Tageslicht. Die großen Erhellungspunkte, von welchen ein
daylight. The large illuminating points, from which an

auf neu entdeckte Weise hergestelltes Licht ausging, waren
on new discovered manner manufactured light went out were
again

in Tätigkeit versetzt worden und warfen ihre Strahlen
in activity set become and threw their rays (of light)

über die Straßen, dass durch die Fenster hindurch selbst
over the streets, that through the window through even

das Innere der Gebäude genügend erhellt wurde. Das
the inner (part) of the buildings enough illuminated became The

Odoratorium hatte sich gefüllt. Kein Platz war leer
Odoratorium had itself filled. No place was empty
had

geblieben.
remained

Die Aktien-Gesellschaft für Temperatur-Regulierung, welche
The share company for temperature regulation which

nicht nur die Erwärmung der öffentlichen und privaten
not only the warming of the public and private

Gebäude im Winter, sondern auch die Kühlung im
buildings in the winter but also the cooling in the

Sommer mit Hilfe eines ausgedehnten Röhrennetzes
summer with help of an extensive pipe network

besorgte, hatte trotz des überfüllten Raumes einen
cared for had despite of the crowded space a

angenehmen Wärmezustand hergestellt. Über dem Ododion
pleasant heat condition manufactured Over the Ododion

glänzte unter dem unaufhörlichen Zutritt eines Stromes
shone under the incessant access of a flow

Sauerstoff ein helles Licht, das zugleich eine
(of) oxygen a bright light that at the same time an

außerordentliche Milde besaß und vor einigen Jahren
extraordinary mildness possessed and before some years

von Oxygen selbst erfunden worden war. Die Dampforgel
from Oxygen himself invented become was The steam organ

war geheizt, der Motor stand bereit, welcher die Bälge
was heated the engine stood ready which the bellows

der Riesentrompete in Bewegung versetzen sollte, das
of the giant trumpet in movement offset should the

Orchester stimmte die übrigen Instrumente, die
orchestra *toned* *the* *rest* *(of the) instruments* *the*

Geruchskästen waren in das Ododion eingeschoben.
smell boxes *were* *in* *the* *Ododion* *inserted*

Indessen plauderte das Publikum über den chinesischen
Meanwhile *chatted* *the* *audience* *about* *the* *Chinese*

Krieg, welcher vor anderthalb Stunden wirklich
war *which* *before* *one and a half* *hours* *really*

ausgebrochen war, über Luftwettfahrten, über die neueste
broken out *was* *over* *air races* *over* *the* *newest*

Mode, eine lebende Seerose in einer mit Meerwasser
fashion *a* *living* *water lily* *in* *a* *with* *sea water*

gefüllten Glaskugel auf dem Kopfe zu tragen, und über
filled *glass sphere* *on* *the* *head* *to* *carry* *and* *over*

das Reimertsche Gedicht, dessen Verfasser mit
the *from Rhymer* *poem* *of which* *author* *with*

selbstzufriedener Miene in der ersten Reihe des Saales,
smug *expression* *in* *the* *first* *row* *of the* *hall*

dicht hinter dem Ododion, saß.
close *behind* *the* *Ododion* *sat*

»Ein Juckeplätzchen gefällig?«, fragte Herr Jota-Spinnfaden,
A *Itchy-platelet* *please maybe* *asked* *Mr.* *Iota-Filament*

Fabrikant von Griffbeschlägen für Reinigungspinsel linker
manufacturer *of* *handle fittings* *for* *cleaning brushes* *of left*

Handschuhfingerspitzen, indem er seiner Nachbarin eine
glove fingertips   while he his neighbor a

zierliche Dose präsentierte.
delicate can presented

»Ich bin so frei«, erwiderte dieselbe, nahm eine der
I am so free answered the same took one of the

kleinen schwarzen Linsen zwischen Daumen und Zeigefinger
small black lentils between thumb and index finger

und klebte dieselbe an ihr Kinn.
and stuck the same on her chin

»Ach, die neuste Mode«, sagte der Herr. »Ich bin noch
Oh the latest fashion said the gentleman I am still

einer von den Alten, die ihr Plätzchen zwischen den
one of the old (ones) who their platelet spot between the

Augenbrauen tragen.«
eyebrows wear

»Man sagt aber, dass das Jucketin dort den Augen
One says however that the Itchy there the eyes

schädlich werde.«
harmful will be

»Das glaube ich nicht – ich jucke überhaupt nicht stark,
That believe I not – I itch at all not strong

und diese Plätzchen verflüchtigen sich sehr schnell,
and this platelet spot evaporates itself very fast

schmecken aber sehr gut und erheitern außerordentlich
tastes however very good and cheers up extraordinary

durch ihren angenehmen Reiz.«
through her pleasant charm

»Und wenigstens genieren sie den Nachbar nicht. Wissen
And at least embarrass they the neighbor not Know

Sie, auf dem Wolkenplatz lässt sich ein Südpolarmensch
you on the cloud square lets oneself a Antarctic human

sehen, der raucht!«
see who smokes

»Raucht, wieso?«
Smokes how so

»Ja, wie früher in den alten Zeiten, ein Kraut, das sie
Yes as before in the old times a herb that they

anzündeten und dann den Rauch verschlangen.«
kindle and then the smoke devoure

»Ja, ja, ich erinnere mich, gelesen zu haben – jedoch, ich
Yes yes I remember me read to have – however I

denke, sie bliesen ihn in das Bier und tranken ihn
think she blew him in the beer and drank him
it it

dann?«
then

»Möglich ist es wohl. Man soll ja ähnliche Sitten
Possible is it well One should yes indeed similar manners

noch in den Schneegebirgen von Innen-Afrika finden. Doch
still in the snow mountains from Inner-Africa find Indeed

den Mann müssen Sie sich einmal ansehen.«
the man must you yourself once look at

»Meiner Ansicht nach«, hörte man auf der Bank dahinter
My opinion to heard one on the bench there behind
To my opinion

sprechen, »ist es unmöglich, dass China siegt; denn den
speak is it impossible that China wins then the

amerikanischen Luftspritzen kann nichts widerstehen. Bei
American air spray can nothing resist By

den Proben im vorigen Jahre haben sie auf eine
the tests in the last years have they on a
from

Entfernung von zweihundert Kilometern, wobei also die
distance of two hundred kilometers where-by thus the

Bahn des Luftstroms schon sehr gekrümmt ist, von
track of the airflow already very curved is from

Chicago aus das große Luftobservatorium über dem Lake
chicago out the great air observatory over the lake

Michigan in der Nähe von Sheboygan vollständig
Michigan in the proximity of Sheboygan totally

umgeblasen und in den See geschmettert.«
blown over and in the lake smashed

»Wissen Sie, das ist erstaunlich, das ist wunderbar, das
Know you that is amazing that is wonderful that

kann ich nicht glauben!«
can I not believe

»Bitte – da, was ist das?«
Sorry – there what is that

Aller Augen wandten sich der Tafel der Publikationen
All eyes turned itself the signboard of the publications

zu, welche auch im Odoratorium nicht fehlte. An der
towards which also in the Odoratorium not lacked on the

Stelle, wo vor wenigen Stunden Magnets
spot where before few hours Magnet's
a few hours ago

verhängnisvolles Poem gestanden, erschien jetzt in großen
disastrous poem stood appeared now in great

Lettern die Depesche:
letters the dispatch

»Vom Kriegsschauplatze. Stilles Weltmeer. Die chinesische
From (the) theater of war Silent Ocean The Chinese
Pacific

Luftflotte näherte sich der Küste von Kalifornien. Unsere
air fleet approached itself the coast of california Our

Strand-Luftbatterien auf der ganzen Strecke zwischen
beach air batteries on the whole distance between

Bondega und Humboldt-Bai kamen gleichzeitig zur
bondega and Humboldt-bai came at the same time to the

Wirkung. Erfolg enorm. Gesamte Flotte in einer
effect *Success* *enormous* *Entire* *fleet* *in* *a*
from

Entfernung von 200 bis 250 Kilometern angegriffen,
distance *of* *200* *to* *250* *kilometers* *attacked*

vollständig zerstreut, größtenteils ins Meer geworfen. Der
totally *destroyed* *mostly* *in the* *sea* *thrown* *The*

Rest floh bis Taiwan (Insel Formosa).
rest *escaped* *to* *Taiwan* *island* *Formosa*

St. Francisco, 2371. 192d 16h63,71m
Saint *Francisco* *2371.* *192d* *16h63.71m*

Claps-Shrum, Kriegsminister«
Claps Shrum *war minister*

Man gratulierte sich und begann ziemlich lebhaft zu
One *congratulated* *each other* *and* *began* *rather* *lively* *to*

werden. In diesem Augenblick trat Aromasia ein. Allein.
become *In* *this* *moment* *stepped* *Aromasia* *in* *Alone*

Oxygen führte sie nicht wie gewöhnlich, sein Platz blieb
Oxygen *led* *her* *not* *as* *usual* *his* *place* *remained*

leer. Das machte Aufsehen. Das Publikum wurde still. Die
empty *That* *made* *sensation* *The* *audience* *became* *quiet* *The*

Herren spannten ihre Lichtschirme auf und klappten sie
gentlemen *strained* *their* *light screens* *~~on~~* *and* *clapped* *them*
closed

wieder zu; das war das Zeichen höchsten Applauses.
again *~~to~~* *that* *was* *the* *sign* *(of the) highest* *applause*

Aromasia grüßte mit einer Bewegung beider Hände und
Aromasia greeted with a movement of both hands and

trat an das Ododion.
stepped on the Ododion

Das Konzert begann.
The concert began

Die Dampforgel spielte einen Teil aus einer alten Oper,
The steam organ played a piece from an old opera

welche im neunzehnten Jahrhundert viel Aufsehen
which in the nineteenth century much sensation

gemacht hatte. Die Klangfarbe der Dampforgel eignete
made had The timbre of her steam organ suited

sich dazu vorzüglich, und das Stück fand Beifall, obgleich
itself there-to excellent and the piece found applause as well as

der neumittelalterliche Text mit seinen Naturlauten viel
the neo-medieval text with its natural sounds much

Heiterkeit erregte.
cheerfulness excited

Nun folgte eine Ododionpiece mit Musikbegleitung. Alle
Now followed an Ododionpiece with music accompaniment All

sperrten im wahren Sinne des Wortes, und
locked in the true sense of the words and
(sperrten auf; wide opened)

mit Recht, Nase und Ohren auf. Aromasia berührte die
with right nose and ears up Aromasia touched the
justly so

Tasten.
keys

Anfänglich herrschte die Musik vor, und Aromasia
initially ruled the music ~~before~~ and Aromasia
prevailed

brauchte nur einen Geruch anzuschlagen, dann den zweiten
needed only a smell to strike then the second

und sie auszuhalten. Aber schon beim ersten verzog sich
and her to endure But already at the first pulled itself

ihr schönes Gesicht – sie musste niesen.
her beautiful face – she had to sneeze

Und so ging es dem ganzen Auditorium. Ein wahrer
And so went it the whole auditorium A truer

Nieskrampf brach aus, so scharf war der Geruch, welcher
sneezing broke out so sharp was the smell which

sich durch den Saal verbreitete. Da trat mit der
itself through the hall spread There stepped with the
added

zweiten Taste ein mephitischer Missduft zu dem ersten –
second button a more mephitic miss-scent to the first –

vergeblich fuhren die baumwollenen Luftsiebe des
in vain drove the cotton air screens of the

Publikums an die Nasen. Aromasia wurde verwirrt und
audience to the noses Aromasia became confused and

bleich. Magnet war schon bei dem ersten scharfen Geruch
pale Magnet was already at the first sharp smell

aufgesprungen und in ihre Nähe geeilt, wo er auf dem
jumped up and in her proximity hurried where he on the

leeren Platze Oxygens sich niederließ. Jetzt wollte er sie
empty place of Oxygen himself settled Now wanted he her

fortführen. Aber noch einmal versuchte die erschreckte
lead away But still once tried the startled

Künstlerin das Ododion. Eine Geruchsleiter perlte unter
artist the Ododion A olfactory pearled under

ihren Fingern und schloss mit einem starken Vielgeruch –
her fingers and lock with a strong great smell –

da war es, als wenn alle bösen Geister aus dem Reiche
there was it as when all bad spirits from the kingdom

der Gase losgelassen seien. Keine menschliche Nase
of the gases released were No human nose

konnte diesen Gestank ertragen!
could this stink endure

Das Publikum schrie, wütete und drängte zum Ausgang.
The audience cried raged and pushed to the exit

Die Musiker warfen ihre Instrumente fort und
The musicians threw her instruments away and

verschwanden durch ihre Privattür. Magnet versuchte die
disappeared through their private door Magnet tried the

ohnmächtige Aromasia emporzuheben. Da ließ ein
passed out Aromasia to lift up There let a

wohlmeinender Techniker den Dampf der Dampforgel
more well-meaning technician the steam of the steam organ

ausströmen, um der verunreinigten Luft entgegenzuwirken.
emanate for the contaminated air to counteract

Aber seine gute Absicht schlug fehl. Es gab ein Getöse,
But his good intention struck wrong It gave a roar
                          failed There was

Gezisch und Gepfeife, welches die Verwirrung noch
hissing and whistle which the confusion even

grausiger machte. Das Publikum glaubte, die höchste
more horrible made The audience believed the highest

Gefahr sei nahe gerückt, und in der Besorgnis um das
danger be close moved and in the concern for the

eigene Leben kannte man keine Rücksicht. Nur einen
own life knew one no consideration Only one

Augenblick richtete sich Magnet empor, um von den Gasen
moment arranged itself Magnet up for from the gas

und Dämpfen nicht selbst betäubt zu werden. Aber schon
and vapors not himself dazed to become But already

hatte ihn der hinausdrängende Menschenstrom erfasst und
had him the pushing out stream of people grasped and

ließ ihn nicht aus seiner Flut. Rasch sah er sich zum
let him not from their flood Quickly saw he himself to the

Ausgange gestoßen. Da, plötzlich ein erschütternder Knall
exit pushed There suddenly a more devastating bang

- ein Teil der entfesselten Gase hatte sich untereinander
- a part of the unleashed gases had itself among itself

und mit der Sauerstoffmenge des Beleuchtungsapparates so
and with the amount of oxygen of the lighting apparatus so

unglücklich gemischt, dass eine starke Explosion erfolgte.
unfortunately mixed that a robust explosion took place

Das Gebäude wankte, die Decke schien sich heben zu
The building wavered the ceiling seemed itself lift to

wollen, doch zum Glück hielt sie stand. Die Menschen
want indeed to the fortune held she stood The people
kept she herself up

waren allmählich durch die Ausgänge entkommen und bis
were gradually through the exits escaped and until

auf wenige gerettet. Aber im Innern wütete ein
on few rescued But in the inside raged a

furchtbarer Brand und lohte zu den Fenstern hinaus.
terrible fire and blazed to the windows out

Im Augenblicke war jetzt durch die Hilfe von außen das
in the moment was now through the help from outside the

erschreckte Publikum aus der unmittelbaren Nähe des
startled audience from the immediate proximity of the

brennenden Gebäudes gebracht. Schon war die
burning building brought Already was the

Brandabteilung der Behörde für öffentliche Sicherheit zur
fire department the authority for public security at the

Stelle, und ihre Exstinktspritzen, welche von dem
spot and their extinct syringes which from the

getroffenen Gegenstande jeden Sauerstoff absperrten, hatten
hit objects every oxygen closed off had

im Nu die Flammen bewältigt. Nun aber, nachdem der
in the now the flames mastered Now however after the

erste Schrecken vorüber war, ging die bange Frage
first fright over was went the frightened question

durch die Menge: Wo ist Aromasia?
through the mass/people Where is Aromasia

Man rief, man suchte. Niemand hatte sie gesehen, sie
One called one searched nobody had her seen she

musste noch im Gebäude sein.
must still in the building his

»Sie ist verbrannt«, schrie Magnet mit der Stimme des
She is burned cried Magnet with the voice of the

Verzweifelnden. »Sie muss verbrannt sein – es war
desperate She must burnt be – it was

unmöglich, die Ohnmächtige zu retten. Doch vielleicht ist
impossible the passed out one to save Indeed perhaps is

noch Hoffnung – hinein ins Odoratorium!«
still hope – inside in the Odoratorium

Die Rettungsmänner versuchten in ihren feuersicheren
The rescue men/rescuers tried in their fireproof

Anzügen das glühend heiße Gebäude zu betreten. Ihnen
clothing the glowing hot building to enter Them

zuvor kam ein Fremder; der Mann, der in seinem gegen
before came a stranger the man who in his against

110

jede Wärme undurchdringlichen Feuerwams nicht zu
each warmth impenetrable fire jerkin not to

erkennen war, brach sich Bahn in den mit Trümmern
recognize was broke himself track in the with ruins
a way

gefüllten Saal. Aber während noch die Rettungsleute im
filled hall But while still the rescue people in the

Saale aufräumten, erschien er schon wieder oben auf der
hall cleaned up appeared he already again above on the

äußeren Galerie, welche das ganze Odoratorium-Gebäude
outer gallery which the whole Odoratorium building

nach der Stadt zu umgab. Auf der östlichen Seite
towards the city towards surrounded On the eastern side

bemerkte man einen Luftmotor, den einige für den des
noticed one an air motor which some for that of the

Warm-Blasius hielten. Neben demselben schien noch ein
Warm-Blasius held Besides the same seemed still a

kugelförmiger Apparat sich zu befinden, doch konnte man
more spherical machine itself to locate indeed could one

denselben nur undeutlich erkennen, er schien von einer
the same only indistinct recognize he seemed from a
it

durchsichtigen Materie zu sein. Jetzt beschäftigte sich der
transparent matter to be Now employed himself the

Unbekannte mit demselben – er stieg hinein, er öffnete
unknown man with the same – he rose inside he opened

einen Hahn. Gespannt schaute man auf sein Beginnen.
a lever Anxiously looked one on his beginning
actions

Da richtete der Fremde sich auf und rief mit lauter,
There arranged the stranger himself up and called with loud

durchdringender Stimme hinunter zu der Menge:
penetrating voice down to the mass
people

»Vernehmt die Trauerkunde! Aromasia ist verbrannt. Suchet
Hear the funeral notice Aromasia is burnt Seek

nicht nach ihrem Mörder – nicht die Erde, nicht die
not to her murderers – not the earth not the

Sonnen haben noch Gewalt über ihn.«
sun have still power over him

Der so gerufen hatte, bückte sich und drehte eine
The one who so called had bent himself and turned a

Handhabe. Eine Kugel schloss sich um ihn, sie begann
handle A bullet closed itself around him she began

zu leuchten – in demselben Augenblick aber flog auch
to shine – in the same moment however flew also

die Kugel, ohne einen sichtbaren Anstoß erhalten zu
the bullet without a visible on-push become to
kickoff

haben, mit rapider Geschwindigkeit von der Galerie des
have with rapid speed from the gallery of the

Odoratoriums in die Nacht hinaus.
Odoratorium in the night away out

Ins All verbannt

Oxygen hatte, am Fenster des Odoratoriums mit seinem
Oxygen had at the window of the Odoratorium with his

Luftmotor haltend, die Katastrophe beobachtet, deren
air motor holding the catastrophe observed which / of which the

schrecklichen Ausgang er nicht gewollt hatte. Magnet sollte
horrible exit/ending he not wanted had Magnet should

durch einen wohlberechneten Gasstrom bläulich angehaucht
through a well calculated gas flow bluish blown at

werden, eine Farbe, die er mehrere Monate
become a colour that he multiple months

behalten hätte, und Aromasia sollte durch die
keep had / would have to keep and Aromasia should through the

Enttäuschung ihrer Nase und den Zorn des Publikums das
disappointment of her nose and the anger of the audience the

Geruchsklavier gründlich verleidet werden. Beides war
Smell-piano thoroughly suffer / start to dislike become Both was / had

vereitelt worden.
foiled become

Im Augenblicke, als die Detonation eintrat, durchzuckte
In the moment as the detonation in-stepped / occurred through twitched

Oxygen das Bewusstsein seiner Tat. Die Folgen seines
Oxygen the awareness of his deed The consequences of his

Beginnens standen vor seiner erschreckten Seele.
beginning stood before his startled soul
actions

Aromasia vernichtet! Mit ihr vielleicht noch Hunderte von
Aromasia destroyed With her perhaps still hundreds of

Menschen! Und durch seine Schuld! Ein tiefer Schmerz
people And through his guilt A deep pain
fault

überkam ihn, aber Oxygen verlor nicht seine Besinnung.
overcame him but Oxygen lost not his sense(s)

Er musste retten, was in seiner Kraft stand. Er eilte
He had to save what in his power stood He hurried
whatever he could

nach Hause, um seinen feuerfesten Anzug zu holen und
to (the) house for his fireproof suit to get and

für alle Fälle...
for all cases
just in case

In die wenigen Augenblicke, deren er bedurfte, um nach
in the few moments which he needed for to

seiner Wohnung zu fliegen, das Rettungswams
his house to fly the rescue jerkin

umzuwerfen und samt seinem geheimnisvollen
around-to-throw and together with his mysterious
to throw over himself

Apparate auf dem Dache des Odoratoriums zu erscheinen,
machine on the roof of the Odoratorium to appear

drängte sich eine solche Fülle von Empfindungen,
pushed itself a such abundance of sensations

Überlegungen, Schlüssen und Entwürfen zusammen, wie nur
considerations conclusions and designs together as only

ein so bevorzugter Geist jener vorgeschrittenen Zeit so
a so advanced spirit in that advanced time so

rasch sie bewältigen konnte. Wenn Aromasia wirklich durch
quickly she master could When Aromasia really through

ihn vernichtet war – das Liebste, was ihn neben seiner
him destroyed was – the dearest that him beside his

Wissenschaft ans Leben fesselte? Wenn er sich selbst
science to the life captivated When he himself self

ihrer Ermordung anklagen musste? Was war die nächste,
her assassination accuse had to What was the next

äußerliche Folge? Dass seine Unvorsichtigkeit das
external consequence That his carelessness the
formal

Unglück herbeigeführt habe, konnte nicht verborgen
misfortune brought about have could not concealed

bleiben. Auch lag es ihm fern, seine Schuld verheimlichen
remain Also lay it him far his guilt to conceal

zu wollen. Das Fachgericht musste ihn schuldig finden der
to want The specialist court had to him guilty find the

vorsätzlichen Beschädigung von Privateigentum, der
intentional damage of private property the

versuchten Körperverletzung und der fahrlässigen Tötung
tried bodily-harm and the negligent killing

von fünf Personen. Er konnte auf zwei bis drei Monate
of five people He could on two to three months
for

115

Einzelhaft rechnen, und die öffentliche Meinung
solitary confinement count and the public opinion

mochte das Urteil durch eine mehrjährige Verbannung
might the judgement through a more-year exile

verschärfen. Und wenn die Zeit vorüber war? Wohl musste
sharpen And when the time past was Well must

er seine gesetzmäßige Strafe und ihre Ableistung, seiner
he his lawful punishment and her performance his

Auffassung und der seiner Zeit nach, als eine
view and the of his time (according) to as a

vollständige Sühne für alles Geschehene auffassen.
complete atonement for everything happened understand

Kein Tadel mehr haftete an ihm. Aber konnte er sich
No blame (any)more clung on him But could he himself

selbst damit zufrieden geben? Konnte er je die
self there-with satisfied give Could he already the
satisfy

Schuld büßen, die er vor seinem Gewissen auf sich
guilt atone which he before his conscience on himself

geladen, dadurch, dass er Aromasia der schrecklichen
loaded there-through that he Aromasia the horrible
through that

Gefahr aussetzte allein um der Befriedigung seiner
danger set out alone for the satisfaction of his

Wünsche willen? Und konnte er je den Verlust
desire's will And could he already the loss

116

verschmerzen,   der   ihm   selbst   als   die   grausamste   Strafe
ache   which him   self   as   the   cruelest   punishment
bear

zugefallen   war,   den   Verlust   der   Geliebten?
fallen to   was   the   loss   of the   beloved (one)
dealt

Ja,   sie   war   grausam,   allzu   grausam,   diese   Strafe!   Was
Yes   she   was   horrible   all too   horrible   this   punishment What

hatte   er   denn   getan,   um   solches   Elend   zu   verdienen?   Was
had   he   then   done   for   such   misery   to   earn   What

jeder   andere   getan   hätte,   der,   gereizt   wie   er,   die   Mittel
each   other   done   had   who   irritated   as   he   the   means

der   Vergeltung   besessen.   Hatte   er   nicht   das   Recht,   auf
of the   retribution   possessed   Had   he   not   the   right   on

Aromasia   einzuwirken,   um   ihre   Neigung,   deren   Verlust   ihm
Aromasia   in-to-work   for   her   inclination which   loss   him
            to influence   affection

drohte,   wiederzugewinnen,   indem   er   die   Feinde   derselben
threatened   to regain   while   he   the   enemy   of the same

beseitigte.   Was   ist   das   für   ein   erbärmliches   Geschick,   was
eliminated   What   is   thta   for   a   pathetic   fate   what

für   eine   unfertige   Weltordnung,   die   auf   so   lächerlich
for   an   unfinished   world order   which   on   so   ridiculous

unbedeutende   Ursachen   hin   so   entsetzliche   Folgen
insignificant   causes   away   so   appalling   consequences

häufen   konnte?
accumulate   could

117

Was bin ich diesem Schicksal und meinem Leben noch
What am I this fate and my life still

schuldig – so sprach er bei sich –, wenn es selbst
owing – so spoke he by himself –, when it even

gegen mich so ungerecht ist, wenn ich ohnmächtig der
against to me so unfair is, when I powerless the

Spielball blinder Gewalten sein soll? Oder dürfen etwa
game ball (of) blind forces be should Or may just
plaything

gewisse Arten des Glücks mir entzogen werden, weil
certain kinds of the happiness me withdrawn become because
taken away

mir einige andere Gaben verliehen sind? Gut, so will ich
me some other gifts awarded are Good so want I

ohne Rücksicht auf Glück und Liebe und Leben Gebrauch
without consideration on fortune and love and life use

von ihnen machen und ihre Wirkungsfähigkeit bis in alle
from them make and her effectiveness until in all

Konsequenzen verfolgen!
consequences follow

Nicht vergebens will ich dein erstes Grundgesetz
Not in vain will I your first basic law

bezwungen haben, du stolze Natur – vom Gesetze der
conquered have you proud nature – from the laws the

Schwerkraft vermag ich einzelne Arten des Stoffes zu
gravity was able I single species of the fabric to

emanzipieren. Ja, mühevoller Arbeit von Jahren ist es
emancipate Yes (with) troublesome work of years is it

gelungen, den molekularen Zustand gewisser chemischer
succeeded the molecular status (of) certain chemical

Zusammensetzungen so zu modifizieren, dass sie der
compositions so to modify that she the

Gravitation nicht mehr fähig sind. Längst wissen wir,
gravitation not (any)more capable of are Long know we

dass es anziehende, durch den leeren Raum wirkende
that it attracting through the empty space acting

Kräfte nicht gibt; der Druck des Weltäthers, dessen
forces not gives the pressure of the world ether which
are

Atome von allen Seiten, doch mit wechselnder Häufigkeit,
atoms from all sides indeed with changing frequency

anprallen, ist es, welcher die Körper nach einem
bounce is it which the body to a

gemeinschaftlichen Schwerpunkt drängt. Für diese
common heavy-point pushes For this
mass

Bewegungsart der Ätheratome habe ich meinen Apparat
type of movement of the ether atoms have I my machine

durchdringbar gemacht, keine Schwerkraft mehr vermag
penetrable made no gravity (any)more is able

ihn zu beeinflussen - und mich selbst? Was macht es,
him to influence - and me myself What makes it
it matters

wenn mein Körper dabei zu Grunde geht? Frei kann ich
when my body there-by to ground goes Free can I
is destroyed

sein, frei will ich sein! Da steht meine Hohlkugel - ein
be free want I be There stands my hollow sphere - a

119

paar Handgriffe, fort schießt sie, von der Schwungkraft
few handles away shoots she from the momentum

der Erde geschleudert, der Schwere enthoben, fort von
of the earth hurled the weight from lifted away from
relieved of

der Oberfläche des Planeten, von seiner Bahn um die
the surface of the planet from its track around the

Sonne, an die sie nichts mehr fesselt. Wohlan, ich
sun on which she nothing (any)more binds Well-on I
Well

schaffe sie auf den Kranz des Odoratoriums; und ist das
create she on the wreath of the Odoratorium and is the
it

Schreckliche wahr, ist Aromasia mir genommen – so
horrible (thing) true is Aromasia me taken – so
then

nimm auch mich dahin, unersättliches Nichts! Ich werde
take also me there to insatiable nothing I will

auf eine Weise aus dem Leben gehen wie noch niemand
on a manner from the life go like still no one

zuvor; ich werde schauen, was noch niemand sah; ich
before I will watch what still nobody saw I

werde auf eine wahrhafte Art gen Himmel fahren.
will on a truthful way towards heaven drive
go

Ist es mir nicht gelungen, trotz aller Macht, die ich über
is it me not succeeded despite all power that I over

die Gesetze der Phänomene hatte, jene kleinen Regungen,
the laws of the phenomena had those small emotions

120

die vom Gehirn Aromasias ausgingen, für mich zu
that from the brain of Aromasia went out for me to

gewinnen, konnte ich nicht den Besitz eines Menschen
win could I not the possession of a human

erringen, der doch nur ein Atom ist im All, hatte das
win which indeed only an atom is in the all had the

blinde Schicksal wirklich so viel Gewalt über mich – so
blind fate really so much force over me – so

kann an meiner Existenz nicht viel liegen. Fahre dahin,
can to my existence not much lie Drive there to
be worth

Oxygen, wo keine Sterne mehr durch den Raum
Oxygen where no stars (any)more through the space

wandeln!
stroll

Von solchen Gedanken bewegt, war Oxygen mit seinem
From such thoughts moved was Oxygen with his
By had

Apparat nach dem Odoratorium zurückgekehrt, hatte sich
machine to the Odoratorium returned had himself

in den heißen Bau gestürzt, Aromasias entstellte
in the hot construction rushed Aromasia's disfigured

Reste gefunden und war an sein Fahrzeug zurückgeeilt.
remains found and was on his vehicle hurried back

Hier rief er die Worte zum Volke hinab, die seinen
Here called he the words to the people down that his

traurigen Entschluss verkündeten. Die durchsichtige
sad decision announced The transparent

121

Hohlkugel schloss sich über ihm, das präparierte Gas
hollow sphere / closed / itself / over / him / the / prepared / gas

wurde von der Materie derselben wie von seinem Körper
became / from / the / matter / the same / as / from / his / body

absorbiert, und der Widerstand gegen den anstürmenden
absorbed / and / the / resistance / against / the / charging

Weltäther war gebrochen. Die Erde, welche ihn nicht
world ether / was / broken / The / ground / which / him / not

mehr an sich zog, schleuderte ihren ungetreuen
(any)more / on, towards / itself / pulled / hurled / her, its / unfaithful

Sohn von sich. Der Stoß des Daches gab der
son / from / itself / The / shock / of the / roof / gave / the

abfliegenden Kugel eine langsame Rotation, und leuchtend
departing / bullet / a / slow / rotation / and / bright shining

durchmaß sie in wenigen Minuten die Atmosphäre der
through measured, crossed / she / in / few / minutes / the / atmosphere / of the

Erde, welche schweigend unter ihr die gewohnte Bahn
earth / which / in silence / under / her / the / accustomed / track, course

fortrollte.
rolled away, followed

Es war ein seltsamer Zustand, in welchem Oxygen sich
It / was / a / strange / status / in / which / Oxygen / himself

befand.
found

Die hohle, durchsichtige Kugel, welche ihn umschlossen
The hollow transparent bullet which him enclosed

hielt, war samt ihrem Inhalt in keiner Weise den
held was together with her content in no manner to the

Wirkungen der Schwerkraft unterworfen. Aber nur
effects of the gravity subjected But only

diejenigen Bewegungen, welche eine Durchdringung durch
those movements which a penetration through

den Äther verhinderten, waren abgeändert. Im Übrigen
the ether prevented were modified In the rest

wirkten die molekularen Bewegungen seines Systems in
worked the molecular movements of his systems in

wenig verwandelter Weise fort, aber es besaß keinen
little changed manner away but it possessed no

Schwerpunkt mehr, weder in sich noch in der
heavy-point (any)more neither in itself nor in the
mass

Außenwelt. Jede Muskelbewegung hatte einen Aufruhr aller
outside world Each muscle movement had a revolt of all

Gegenstände im Innern der Kugel zur Folge. Es war
objects in the inside o the bullet to the follow It was

natürlich, dass die Bedingungen des Lebensprozesses
of course that the conditions of the life process

abgeändert wurden, und ehe noch die Atemluft verzehrt
modified became and before still the breathing air digested

war, hatte der Pulsschlag aufgehört. Oxygens reiches Leben
was had the pulse beat stopped Oxygen's rich life

entfloh.
escaped

Sein Fahrzeug aber flog mit der gleichmässigen
His vehicle however flew with the uniform

Geschwindigkeit, welche es als Teil der Erde besessen
speed which it as part of the earth possessed

und in Folge des Beharrungsvermögens der Körper
and in consequence of the perseverance of the body

beibehalten hatte, langsam rotierend durch den
maintained had slowly rotating through the

unermesslichen Raum. Kein Planet, keine Sonne vermochte
immeasurable space No planet no sun could

es aus seiner Bahn zu lenken, kein Meteor erfuhr eine
it from its track to direct no meteor experienced a
draw

Störung durch dasselbe. In unendlicher gerader Linie glitt
disturbance through the same In unending straight line slid

das neue Gestirn durch die ganze Ausdehnung des
the new heavenly object through the whole expansion of the

Sonnensystems, welches unter ihm forteilte, an deren
solar system which under him hurried through on which

Sonnen vorüber, hinaus, hinaus bis in die Nebelfernen,
sun past out out until in the fog-distance

bis in die Unendlichkeit –
until in the infinity –

Die Menge hatte sich verlaufen. Der Verkehr in dem von
The mass had itself run up / spread out The traffic in the from / by

der Katastrophe betroffenen Stadtteil unterschied sich in
the catastrophe affected city-part / district varied itself in

nichts mehr von dem in den entfernteren Gebieten,
nothing (any)more from that in the more distant areas

welche kaum das Unglück gewahr geworden waren. Die
which hardly the misfortune notice become / had noticed were The

Geschäfte nahmen ihren durch die Nacht nur wenig
businesses took their through the night only little

unterbrochenen Gang. Die Erhellungspunkte glühten, die
interrupted course The illuminating points glowed the

Luftwagen schwirrten, in den Vereinslokalen debattierte man
air car whirred in the local clubs debated one

über die Zeitfragen, und in den öffentlichen
about the time issues / questions of that time and in the public

Erholungsstätten klangen die Gläser; noch spendete der
places of rest / recreational facilities sounded the glasses still spilled the

Wein dieselbe göttliche Heiterkeit wie bei den Gelagen
wine with the same divine cheerfulness as at the dinners

der Olympier. Nur allgemeiner war die Freude geworden.
of the Olympians Only more general was / had the joy become

125

Der Strom der Menschheit flutete weiter. Wer vermochte
The flow of the mankind streamed further Who was able

die Stelle zu zeigen, wo die verlorenen Wasserstäubchen
the place to show where the lost water dust particles

fehlten?
were missing

Magnet hatte Oxygen am Klange der Stimme erkannt,
Magnet had Oxygen at the sound of the voice recognized

mit welcher er Aromasias Untergang verkündet hatte. Sein
with which he Aromasia's going down announced had His
doom

Schmerz und seine Trauer duldeten ihn nicht an der
pain and his mourning tolerated him not to the

Stätte, wo ihm eine Welt untergegangen und doch die
site where him a world gone under and indeed the

Welt dieselbe geblieben war. An jenen Ort wollte er eilen,
world the same remained was On that place wanted he rush

wohin ohne das Dazwischentreten eines grausamen
where-to without the There-between-step of a cruel
mixing

Geschicks ihn sonst mit ihr zusammen der Luftwagen
fate him otherwise with her together the air car

getragen hätte. Dort erzählte ihm der gleiche Fortgang
carried had There told him the same progress

des Lebens rings um ihn nichts von der
of the life in a circle around him nothing from the

126

Gleichgültigkeit der Welt; dort hatte ja Aromasia nicht
indifference of the world there had yes Aromasia not
                                    indeed

gelebt, und darum konnte es ihn nicht kränken, dass er
lived and therefore could it him not offend that he

nicht in jedem Auge seinen eigenen Schmerz wieder fand;
not in each eye his own pain again found

dort durfte er seinen Verlust als einen unersetzlichen
there was allowed he his loss as an irreplaceable (one)

betrauern. Im Gebiete der Luft und an den Wassern
mourn In the area of the air and on the water

des Niagara wollte er seinen schmerzlichen Träumen
of the Niagara wanted he his painful dream

nachhängen und in seiner Weise die Versöhnung suchen.
after-hang and in his (own) manner the reconciliation search
follow

Der schwache Schein der Dämmerung im Norden hatte
The weak shine of the dusk in the north had

seinen niedrigsten Stand erreicht, als der Motor Obertons
its lowest stand reached as the engine of Oberton
                level

in die klare Nacht emporstieg. Hinter ihm, unter ihm
in the clear night ascended Behind him under him

blieb die Stadt, blieben die gewöhnten Lande. Es war
remained the city remained the used to lands It was

dem Dichter, als müsse er die ganze Erde hinter sich
the poet as must he the whole earth behind himself

127

zurücklassen und nur in eine ferne Zukunft Sehnsucht
leave behind and only in(to) a distant future desire

und Gedanken richten.
and thoughts aim

Ich verstehe dich, ich begreife dich, Oxygen, dachte er,
I understand you I understand you Oxygen thought he

dass du nicht nur der menschlichen Gesellschaft, dass du
that you not only the human company that you

der Welt selbst Lebewohl gesagt. Ich ahne es, du hast
the world itself live-well said I guess it you have
goodbye

deine Macht über die Kräfte der Natur angewandt, dich
your power over the forces of the nature applied yourself

jeglichem Einflusse derselben zu entziehen. Zum Nullpunkt
any influences of the same to pull away To the zero point

des Seins wolltest du dringen, und für deinen Teil
of the existence wanted you penetrate and for your part

glaubst du die Aufgabe gelöst zu haben. Du hast der
believe you the task solved to have You have the

Schwerkraft, dem großen Bande des Kosmos, dich
gravity the large band of the cosmos yourself

entrissen, frei fliegst du dahin, durch nichts angezogen,
ripped off free fly you there to through nothing drawn

durch nichts geleitet, in absoluter Unabhängigkeit, in einer
through nothing led in absolute independence in a

wahrhaft freiwilligen und unwiderruflichen Verbannung. Ins
truly voluntary and irrevocable exile In the

128

All verbannt! Und doch bist du nicht wahrhaft frei! Du
all banished And indeed are you not truly free You

selbst musst sterben und empfindest schon deine Freiheit
self must die and feels already your freedom

nicht mehr! Aber auch vom großen Verbande des
not (any)more But also from the great relations of the

Seins konntest du dich in Wirklichkeit nicht lösen!
existence could you yourself in reality not loosen

Noch gibt es molekulare Bewegungen und lebendige Kräfte
Still gives it molecular movements and lively forces
      exist

in deinem eigenen Gestirn, die ohne Wirkung nicht im
in your own forehead which without effect not in the

All verschwinden können. Oh, ich folge dir auf deiner
all disappear can Oh I follow you on your

Bahn durch die Sterne, ich eile mit dir in Milliarden von
track through the stars I hurry with you in billions of
course

Jahren vorüber an den Sonnen der Milchstraße, vorüber
years past on the suns of the milky way past
      by

an all den hellen und dunklen Gebilden, welche den Raum
on all the bright and dark shapes which the space
by

in ungemessenen Weiten erfüllen.
in unmeasured widths fulfill

Aber einst – ich sehe es – trifft deine Kugel doch auf
But once – I see it – meets your bullet indeed on

deiner Bahn an eines derselben. Ein chaotischer Weltnebel
your track on one of the same A more chaotic world nebula

ist es, noch im ersten Stadium seiner Bildung, vielleicht
is it still in the first stage of its formation perhaps

das Resultat einer Weltzerstörung. In völliger Trennung
the result of a world destruction In more complete separation

irren die Atome ohne Zusammenhang durch den Raum,
err the atoms without context through the space

noch gibt es keine Wärmebewegung, noch zittert keine
still gives it no heat movement still trembles no

Lichtwelle durch die Nacht. Da tritt deine Kugel hinein
light wave through the night There steps your bullet inside

mit ihrer lebendigen Kraft, und ein Anstoß zu neuen
with her lively strength and a on-push to new
kickoff

Schwingungsarten ist gegeben. In regelmäßig umlaufenden
types of vibration is given In regularly circulating

Bahnen gruppieren sich die Atome zu Molekeln, von ihren
courses group itself the atoms to molecules from their

geordneten Stößen getroffen, erzittert der Äther, und
orderly bumps hit trembles the ether and

Leuchten kommt in die Masse. So wenigstens muss ein
shining comes in the mass so at least must a

Mensch den Vorgang beschreiben. Ich bin nur ein Mensch,
human the process describe I am only a human

aber ich weiß es: Ein neues Gestirn flammt am
but I know it A new heavenly object blazes at the

Himmel auf. Noch sah es die Erde nicht, noch müssen
sky up Still saw it the earth not still must

Jahrtausende vergehen, ehe der Lichtstrahl zur Erde
millennia pass before the beam of light to the earth

gelangt – aber es wird geschehen.
reached – but it will happen

Armer Oxygen, so bist du doch nicht frei, nicht frei von
Poor Oxygen so are you indeed not free not free from

den Banden unentrinnlichen Seins; die Schwere flohest
the bounds inescapable of existence the weight fled

du, und wieder reißen dich die Atome in ihren
you and again tear yourself the atoms in their

Wirbeltanz. Du kanntest nicht den richtigen Weg, den
whirl dance You knew not the true way the

einzigen, den es gibt, von jenen Kräften des Stoffes
only (one) that it gives from those powers of the fabric
there is

sich zu befreien. Der alte Dichter kannte ihn wohl:
oneself to free The old poet knew him well

»Aber dringt bis in der Schönheit Sphäre,
But penetrate until in the beauty sphere

Und im Staube bleibt die Schwere
And in the dust remains the weight
mass

Mit dem Stoff, den sie beherrscht, zurück.«
With the material the she controlled back
ruled

Ja, Oxygen, hier ist Freiheit! Ich bin frei bin es durch
Yes Oxygen here is freedom I am free am it through

die Macht des Ideals, bin es durch meine dichtende
the power of the ideal am it through my rhyming
poetic

Kunst, die mich über die Schranken der Welt und meiner
art that me over the limits of the world and my

räumlichen und zeitlichen Existenz hinausträgt.
spatial and temporal existence carries out

Ha! Durch deinen neuen Stern, den die Folgen deines
Ha Through your new star which the consequences of your

Unrechts hervorriefen, sehe ich die Versöhnung kommen –
injustice evoked see I the reconciliation come –

nicht in einer geträumten Ewigkeit, in einem erdichteten
not in a dreamed eternity in a forged

Jenseits, das frei wäre von den Gesetzen der Natur, die
other-side that free would be from the laws of the nature that

alles binden; sondern, wenn auch in der Dichtung, so
everything bind but when also in the poetry so

doch innerhalb dieser Gesetze, durch die Gewalt
indeed within of these laws through the force

unzerstörbarer Wirkungen im Mechanismus der Welt.
indestructible effects in the mechanism of the world

Tausende von Jahrmillionen gehen dahin, aber die heilige
thousands of millions of years go there to but the holy

Kraft meiner Kunst deutet mir die Versöhnung.
strength of my art points/shows me the reconciliation

Zu der Zeit, da dein Stern aufleuchtet, rollt die Erde
To/At the time there/when your star lights up rolls/turns the earth

vielleicht nicht mehr in ihrer alten Bahn. Hat sich eine
perhaps not (any)more in her old track/course Has itself a

Flutwelle am Sonnenäquator als ein neuer Planet abgelöst
tidal wave at the equator of the sun as a new planet replaced

und ist die Erde mit den Übrigen ein Stückchen weiter
and is the earth with the rest a bit further

hinausgeflogen? Oder haben die hemmenden Kräfte des
flown out Or have the inhibitory forces of the

Ozeans die Rotation der Erde verzögert und ist sie dem
ocean the rotation the earth delayed and is she the

Sonnenball näher gerückt? Sei es so oder so – in jedem
sun ball closer moved Be it so or so – in each

Falle haben sich die Verhältnisse auf ihrer Oberfläche so
case have itself the conditions on her surface so

geändert und mit ihnen die der lebenden Wesen, dass
changed and with them those of the living beings that

wir die alte Menschheit nicht wieder erkennen.
we the old mankind not again recognize

Zwar ein Teil derselben hat auf dem alten Standpunkte
Indeed one part of the same has on the old viewpoints

sich erhalten. Aber es sind unterdrückte Wesen. Eine
itself kept But it are suppressed beings A
        they

vorgeschrittenere Gattung beherrscht den Planeten, und in
more advanced genus controls the planet and in

den mannigfachen Katastrophen ist die Tradition ihrer
the manifold disasters is the tradition of her

Abstammung aus gemeinschaftlicher Wurzel verloren
ancestry from common root lost

gegangen. Von den verachteten Menschen wollen sie
gone From the despised humans want they

nichts wissen. Unvergleichlich höher steht dies Geschlecht
nothing know Incomparably higher stands this generation

mit der schweren Gehirnmasse, mit den Wirbelfüßen und
with the heavy brain mass with the vertebrae and

der komplizierten Organisation, die es sich im Kampfe
the complicated organization which it itself in the fight

ums Dasein erworben hat. Die Zerebrer sind es – ach,
for the there-be acquired has The cerebrer are it – Oh
    existence

Reimert-Oberton, sie kennen deine Werke nicht mehr!
Rhymer-Overtone you know your work not (any)more

Zwischen zwei im Mondlicht glänzenden Abendwolken
Between two in the moonlight glistening evening clouds

lustwandelt ein Zerebrer-Pärchen. Ihre Windmühlenflügelfüße
lustwalks a Cerebral couple Their windmill wing feet

134

bewegen sich so schnell, dass sie die Luft treten. Das
move itself so fast that they (on) the air step The

Thema ihres Gespräches ist nicht neu. Es ist nicht nur
theme of their conversation is not new It is not only

vor zwölf Milliarden Jahren von den Menschen in
before twelve billion years from the people in

glühenden Liedern abgehandelt worden, auch vor ihnen
glowing songs resolved become also before them

schon hatten es die Pterosaurier mit ihren Flughäuten
already had it the pterosaurs with their flight skin

gesäuselt. Denn es dreht sich um die natürliche
whispered Then it turns itself around the natural

Zuneigung zweier Wesen verschiedenen Geschlechts, welche
affection (of) two beings of different gender which

man die Liebe nennt.
one ~~the~~ love calls

Das Pärchen scheint nicht ganz einig zu sein.
The pair seems not completely agreed to be
in agreement

Unwillig runzelt sie die Flugschwimmhaut und achtet nicht
Unwilling frowns she the flying swimming skin and respects not

auf seine flehenden Worte.
on his pleading words

Was hatte er verbrochen? Vielleicht den schönen
What had he broken Perhaps the beautiful

Schraubenfuß einer anderen gelobt? Ach, die Mädchen sind
propellor foot of an other praised Oh the girls are

135

so schwer zu verstehen, und nun gar eine Zerebrin. Kurz
so heavy/hard to understand and now at all a Cerebrin Short

und gut, sie ist ungehalten.
and good she is indignant

Zu seinem Unglück kommt ein Mensch auf seinem
To his misfortune comes a human on his

Luftrade der Ungnädigen zu nahe. Der Windzug stört sie,
air wheel the gracious ones too close The wind pull disturbs her

ein Tritt von ihrem Schraubenfuß, und der Arme stürzt
a step from her propellor foot and the poor (one) crashes

hinab.
down

Wie grausam, braust Herr Zerebrus auf.
How horrible roars Mr Cerebrus up

Es ist ja nur ein Mensch! sagt sie wegwerfend.
It is yes/indeed only a human says she away-throwing/dismissive

Nur ein Mensch? Glaubst du denn, dass ein Mensch nicht
Only a human Believe you then that a human not

auch Empfindung besitzt, denkt und fühlt?
also sensation possesses thinks and feels

Wenn er mich aber inkommodiert?
When he me however discomforts/troubles

So verdient er doch Rücksicht wie jedes lebende Wesen.
So earned he still consideration as any living being

Aus den Menschen erst hat sich unser Geschlecht zu
From the people first has itself our generation to

solcher Vollkommenheit entwickelt, und du kannst nicht
such perfection developed and you can not

wissen, ob du nicht einen Urahnvetter deines
know whether you not a great cousin of your

Geschlechtes verletzt hast.
gender injured have

Jetzt bist du aber unartig, sagte sie zürnend. Von
Now are you however naughty said she angry From

diesen unverständigen Tieren sollen wir abstammen, die
this unwise / senseless animal should we descend who

nur heulen und krächzen können und nicht einmal von
only howl and croak can and not once from

selbst fliegen? Und wir, mit unserer Weltanschauung – ich
itself fly And we with our worldview – I

bitte dich!
ask you

Und doch verstehen sie untereinander ihre Sprache
And indeed understand they among themselves their language

geradeso wie wir die unsere, und wenn sie sich
just like that as we the ours and when they themselves

auch auf einer niederen Entwicklungsstufe befinden, wenn
also on a lower stage of development are found when

137

ihnen auch vielleicht die Anschauung des Unbedingten
them also perhaps the view of the unconditional
to them

abgeht, so fühlen sie den Schmerz wie du und
goes off so feel they the pain like you and
incomprehensible is

freuen sich ihres Lebens wie du; die Empfindung
are pleased themselves of their life like you the sensation

ist relativ und dem Menschen ebenso wertvoll wie dem
is relative and the people likewise valuable as the

Zerebrer. Unrecht ist es daher, ihn zu quälen oder zu
Cerebrals wrong is it there-from him to hurt or to
thus

töten. Vielleicht wartet jetzt vergebens die einsame
kill Perhpaps waits now in vain the lonely

Geliebte auf den Zermalmten.
loved (one) on the crushed (one)

Oh, du bist abscheulich! Mir solche Vorwürfe zu machen
Oh you are hideous Me such reproaches to make

und mit einem Menschen mich zu vergleichen! Du liebst
and with a human me to compare You love

mich nicht! So gehe doch zu deiner einsamen Menschin
me not So go indeed to your lonely human

und tröste sie! Wenn sie so gefühlvoll ist, was brauchst
and comfort her When she so sensitive is what need

du mich? Geh nur!
you me Go only

Was sollte er tun, als um Verzeihung bitten?
What should he do as for forgiveness ask
but

Aber sie war hartnäckig. So rasch geht das nicht, sagte
But she was persistent So quickly goes that not said

sie. Ich weiß nicht, ob ich dir deine Ungezogenheit
she I know not whether I you your naughtiness

vergeben darf. Aber ich will milde sein – ich werde das
forgive may But I want mild be – I will the

Unbedingte fragen.
absolute ask

Er war es zufrieden.
He was it satisfied

Rate einmal, sagte sie, gerade oder ungerade?
Guess once said she even or uneven

Ungerade! rief er.
Uneven called he

Ich habe die Sterne dort oben in dem Quadratgrade
I have the stars there above in the square degrees

gemeint. Nun wollen wir zählen, wie viel es sind. Wer
meant Now want we count how much it are Who
they

wird Recht haben?
will right have
be

Das Zählen war im Nu geschehen; denn sie waren
The count was in the now happened then they were

Zerebrer.
Cerebrals

Gerade! sagte sie.
Even said she

O weh! klagte der verurteilte Liebhaber! Doch nein!
O woe complained the condemned lover Indeed no

rief er jetzt, ungerade! Zähle noch einmal!
called he now odd Count still once

Wahrhaftig, eben ist ein neuer Stern aufgeleuchtet – die
Truly just is a new star lit up – the

Liebe war gerettet.
love was rescued

Das war dein Stern, Oxygen!
That was your star Oxygen

Die Zerebrer schüttelten sich gerührt die Mittelhände.
The Cerebrals shook themselves touched the middle hands

Magnet war bei diesen Fantasien ruhig sind fast heiter
Magnet was at this fantasy calm are almost cheerful
had

geworden.
become

Am   Falle   des   Niagara   senkte   sich   sein   Wagen.
at the   (water)fall   of the   niagara   lowered   itself   his   carriage

»Ich   hab's   gefunden!«,   rief   er   aus.   »Das   ist   der   Entwurf
I   have it   found   called   he   out   That   is   the   design

zu   meinem   neuesten   Roman!«
to   my   latest   novel

Die   Arbeit   ließ   ihn   seinen   Schmerz   vergessen.
The   work   let   him   his   pain   forget

Selbstzufrieden   telegrafierte   er   an   seinen   Verleger   in
Satisfied with himself   telegraphed   he   on   his   publisher   in

Europa: »Was   bieten   Sie   ungesehen   für   meinen   neuesten
Europe   What   offer   you   unseen   for   my   latest

Roman   ›Das   Zerebrer-Pärchen   oder   Der   gezähmte
novel   The   Cerebral couple   or   The   tamed

Lichtnebel‹?«
light fog

»Fünfzigtausend   Münzeinheiten!«,   lautete   die   Antwort.
Fifty thousand   coin units   read   the   answer

»Angenommen!«
Accepted

Magnet   ließ   sich   vor   einem   der   großen   Hotels   nieder,
Magnet   let   himself   before   one   of the   large   hotels   down

auf   einem   Platze,   von   welchem   sich   die   herrlichste
on   a   place   from   which   itself   the   most gorgeous

Aussicht auf den Fall bot, und fing sogleich zu
view on the fall offered and caught immediately to
(fing an: started)

schreiben an. Natürlich telegrafisch.
write on Of course telegraphically

Die Sonne ging auf und bildete glänzende Regenbogen
The sun went up and formed shiny rainbows

im Wasserstaube des Riesenfalls.
in the water dust of the huge fall

»Versöhnt durch zerstörte Liebe ward neue Liebe in
Reconciled through destroyed love became new love in

fernem Geschlecht.« So schrieb Magnet, und der
(a) distant generation So wrote Magnet and the

gehorsame Ätherstrom trug die Worte durch den Leib
obedient ether stream carried the words through the body

des Erdballs nach Europa. Sie standen in der
of the earthball to Europe They stood in the

Abendzeitung neben Aromasias Nachruf.
evening news beside Aromasia's obituary

Made in the USA
Las Vegas, NV
16 October 2023

79229010R00085